A Darker

Shade of

Blue

....

Anthology of poems written by people struggling with their mental health and also by the loved ones of people struggling - to give them a voice, to raise awareness and to raise money to provide complementary therapies to people in emotional crisis and on a low income

Tracey Ward

About Tracey Ward

Tracey Ward is the founder of Harrogate Black Dog, an online community of people struggling with all kinds of mental health from all ages and backgrounds. It is a place where people can talk openly and safely with people who understand and without being judged or criticised or ridiculed. Some of the members are also the loved ones of people struggling so that they can get an insight into what their loved ones are experiencing. Tracey is constantly trying to raise awareness for mental health and is something she is very passionate about.

Tracey went on to set up Karma Times CIC in March of 2020. The aim of this not for profit is to raise money to provide complementary therapies to people in emotional crisis and on a low income.

Tracey, a Complementary Therapist and originally from Leicester, moved to Harrogate in 1997 to study for her degree in Art and Design at Leeds Metropolitan University, graduating with a first class honours. She also appeared in an ITV documentary in 2018 called The Fast Fix: Diabetes and has been featured in numerous newspapers and several magazines along the way.

Tracey is an artist, author, a podcaster, a lifestyle blogger/ influencer, Mental Health First Aider, and Managing Director of Karma Times CIC.

A Darker Shade of Blue

Foreward

At the time of this book's publication, the United Kingdom, along with the rest of the world, finds itself in the grip of a pandemic. A silent killer that does not discriminate and strikes with unrelenting ferocity. Whilst, understandably, the world's media features this pandemic with justifiable prominence it should not detract from that other pandemic that blights so many of our lives. It, too, is a silent killer which does not discriminate and renders its victims helpless with fear and anxiety.

I am, of course, talking about mental health. The black dog, melancholy, depression or whatever you choose to call it. It is with some dismay that I note that the media do not feature this pandemic with such high importance. Indeed, all too often mental health is regarded as a taboo subject. A prohibited topic of conversation, one that should not be discussed in polite company, a subject that should be swept under the carpet. People's inability or unwillingness to talk about mental health can often be as cruel as the affliction itself.

There are, however, many other people who recognise mental health issues and the importance of talking about them. The editor of this anthology, Tracey Ward, is one of those people. She set up the Harrogate Black Dog, an online support group for mental health awareness a number of years ago and her passion and tireless commitment for maintaining that awareness has culminated in this collection of poems written by people either suffering from mental health issues or by the loved ones of people who are suffering.

I am sure I am not the only person to have found solace in the words of others, be it in stories, novels, poems or prose. Every single one of this book's contributors should be applauded for their courage and their bravery in laying bare their innermost thoughts, emotions and feelings.

It is my firm belief that the words contained within these pages will make the reader realise that there really is light beyond those dark tunnels of depression and that it is always okay to not feel okay.

If this collection of poems makes just one person reach out, seek help and inspire them to work on their self-worth and self-belief then it will have achieved its aim.

Steve Markham, Author

January 2021

A Darker Shade of Blue

A Darker Shade of Blue

First published in Great Britain in 2021 by Amazon KDP

Copyright Tracey Ward 2021

First Edition

A CIP catalogue record for this title is available from the British Library.

A Darker Shade of Blue

In a world where you can be anything; be kind...

Caroline Flack

Table of Contents

In loving memory of all the people that have sadly taken their own life; not just in the United Kingdom but all over the world.

I also dedicate this book to all of the loved ones left behind and to everyone affected by the sad loss of victims of suicide.

Introduction

I'm just going to come out with it; I don't care what anyone says the fact is we all struggle with our mental health at some point in our lives. Anyone who says that they don't is not being honest with themselves and I'm sorry but that's the truth and sadly, some people just don't want to admit to it and that is their right too; because denial is more than likely their coping mechanism.

Depression, stress and anxiety affect people in so many different ways not just emotionally but physically too. Sadly, depression is something I've struggled with for most of my life. I have experienced one hell of a lot of bad life experiences and events and I guess you can only cope with so much before you start to break. Murder of school friends and living alongside a serial killer, divorce, rape, sexual abuse, physical abuse, emotional abuse, chronic illnesses, severe anxiety the list is endless. Unfortunately for me, it felt like one hell of a long rollercoaster ride but with more dips than highs. I've been on various medications for this over the years; had counselling and talking therapy. It works to some degree but its not for some people.

Depression can turn you into a recluse, you stop opening post, you stop answering the phone, you stop opening the curtains, you sleep all day, you eat rubbish and lots of it, you don't leave the house, you don't wash, you're wearing pj's 24/7, you stop putting make up on, you start to vegetate and once you are in that state you don't have the ability to get out of it; well you think you don't; I'm living proof that you can.

Five years ago I was in a bad place and was on a serious downward spiral. I'd just been diagnosed with fibromyalgia so feeling incredibly poorly, I was in a relationship which had left me having to sleep on the living room floor for 8 months, no privacy, my life was taken over by my "boyfriend" and his daughter who completely trashed my bedroom. It was a living hell.

In fact if I think about it every single relationship I've had with a man since moving up North in 1997 has been abusive. But.. I am not bitter. Life has a way of giving you the best gifts disguised as your worst experiences. My life experiences mean that I can help others. I understand anguish, despair, desperation, sadness and loneliness. It has given me compassion and empathy and the desire and deep craving to help others and the strength to do it.

During my worst times I started writing down my feelings which soon developed into poems. Now I hadn't written a poem since I was at school about 200 years ago so it was a bit out of the blue. However, it was so cathartic. On completion of each piece of writing I felt like a huge weight had been lifted off my shoulders. I'm no writing expert and I'm certainly no poet laureate but that isn't what I am aiming for. I was just giving my heart a voice and a way to offload. This is when it dawned on me that I should try and encourage other people to do the same thing and see if it helps them the way it has helped me. Not only that I thought it would be a great way of showing the world what mental illness feels like to someone suffering and increasing awareness but also hopefully helping people at the same time.

This book is not a writing competition, the poems are not to be judged, or critiqued each single one is as important as the next. This book is giving people who are struggling a voice; a voice that needs to be heard and will be dedicated to the people who sadly take their own lives.

Before lockdown and the Covid-19 pandemic over 18 people committed suicide in this country every single day and that is 18 people too many. The devastation it leaves behind is immense and the sad thing is this number is rising. The Covid-19 pandemic is also creating more and more people who are struggling with their mental health and all ages.

According to the Samaritans the things that are increasing are negative thoughts about the future, people are experiencing uncertainty, fear and concerns about what the future holds with regards to income and job loss etc. Also people who used to rely on community support and meetings with friends have been diminished or unavailable. This is causing a greater level of distress as time goes on. Sometimes, loss is coming from multiple angles all at once, which is particularly difficult for people to cope with.

A lot of people have been struggling with the extra time alone and at home. This can lead to "overthinking" or having cyclical thought processes. In some instances, this related to previous traumatic experiences or memories that had re-emerged during lockdown. The Samaritans also stated that a small number of callers spoke to them about feeling like a burden to families and friends during lockdown and also do not want to burden the NHS with their mental and physical health.

Ultimately and sadly the pandemic is going to be causing problems with mental health for a long time and we need to start doing something about it immediately.

This book is giving people a voice; a voice that needs to be heard. In return we need to reach out our hands and do whatever we can to help.

This anthology is not going to be easy reading but it is honest, and comes from the heart.

To everyone who has submitted poems for the book I thank you from the bottom of my heart and am so touched by your openness, your bravery and your strength. You inspire me every single day.

Thank you

Tracey

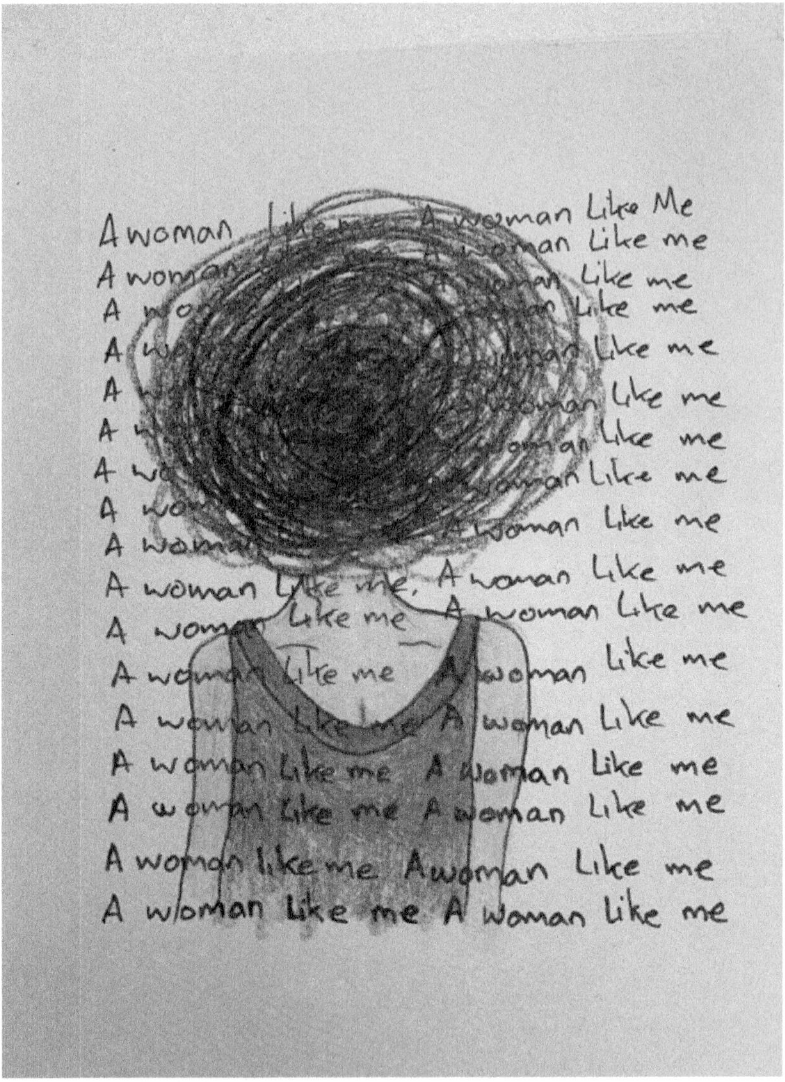
A woman Like Me
A woman Like me
A woman Like me
A woman Like me
A woman Like me
A woman Like me
A woman Like me A woman Like me
A woman Like me A woman Like me
A woman Like me A woman Like me
A woman like me A woman Like me
A woman Like me A woman Like me

Chapter 1

Poems

"If you know someone who's depressed, please resolve never to ask them why. Depression isn't a straightforward response to a bad situation; depression just is, like the weather."

- Stephen Fry

THE ROBBED THAT SMILES, STEALS SOMETHING FROM THEIR THIEF

A split-second tsunami leaves her

clinging to the precipice.

Her thoughts, zooming, spinning, tangling,

like dirty laundry on a full washing cycle.

Clawing her way out of darkness,

as life flashes through her mind.

Is this the penalty of letting her guard down?

she whispers in exhaustion.

A split-second is all the thief needed.

Her back turned momentarily, at the time

that she was nursing her sick child.

Possessions pilfered. Dreams on hold.

She lies confused, imprisoned in turmoil,

as wounds and scars embed below the surface.

Anchored chains weighing her down,

draining her mind, body, and soul.

In a split-second, her belief brings inner strength.

Manifestation to break off the links, and through

meditation; cleansing, healing, growing, and

paving her way in light to her true life's purpose.

For, they will never imprison her mind.

They will certainly not leave her physically broken.

Nor shall they steal her mental health, ever.

Her tide will turn as sure as night follows day!

By Nirmal Kaur Orjally

ANOTHER YOU

This Mother's Day will be the last.

Not for life but something past.

A tiny stroke has robbed you huge.

But I will find you in there applying rouge.

Do your homework, make your bed.

It's my turn now to stroke your head.

No more goodnights or kisses to sleep.

Just me and you thinking of diving deep.

A new day and a new you arrives.

It's surprising and good and I hope it survives.

Closer than ever as your identity rises.

I hope it brings a few more surprises.

Now Autumn rolls in and a new normal prevails.

And you start to remember fond memories and tales.

Days of sunshine and laughter start to become clear.

And I see you in there again my darling mother dear.

By Anna Murphy

Note- this poem is dedicated to my darling mother who suffered a stroke during lockdown, was gone for a while but now finding her way back to her self and me.

MISCHIEF MAKERS

Two little girls,

The shadow of each other.

Confident together,

With protection from their brother.

Differ in ways,

Like night and day.

Yet similar souls

Within siblings play.

Imaginary worlds,

They become risk takers.

Strangers looking in

Just see mischief makers.

Mischievous smiles far removed,

From feeling so dejected.

In their imaginary world,

Now totally protected.

Just two broken souls,

Not serious law breakers.

Learning to live again,

Through being mischief makers.

By Tracey Hand

THE MASK

The social facade

Smiles and laughter,

To watch genuine happiness-

It's much sought after.

Retire to the place I call home,

The deadly silence of being alone.

I remove the mask.

A hurt that's been forever inside,

Is pushed back to the surface-

My personality divide.

A solitary life.

Friends are few and sparse,

A life lived out in public-

Nothing but a farce.

Alone for hours, days.

Silence surrounds me,

Why think of love

When the wrong love found me.

The sun awakens me and my thoughts

As I bask,

Another day beckons,

As I reach for my mask.

By Tracey Hand

WHAT IS REAL?

Friendship that ends with a blink of the eye?

That ends for what reason?

You can't explain why.

That leaves you mistrusting, next time one comes by.

The love of a man who betrays and deceives you,

That no one around you either sees or believes you.

Utter distraught that overwhelms and never leaves you.

The love of your child, who's words cut like a knife,

When times feel like trouble and sadness is rife.

That someone you've given to all of your life.

A job you excel in, but never get credit.

A life of hard working but instead it is

Basically a life you just want to edit.

What is real?

By Tracey Hand

CHANGE

Ugly caterpillar, trusting, twisting, lonesome, creeping,

Frightened, worried, stressed, unloved.

Only escapism is sleeping.

The world around is huge and scary,

People, sounds - everything makes her wary.

Imposing people looking down on this pathetic creature.

It's destructive behaviour is its only defensive feature.

Over time the self disgust vanishes but next comes an explosion.

People now look in awe, as they witness exclusion.

Butterfly flutters by and looks down on the view,

Of the hurters and the doubters,

Of a life it once knew.

By Tracey Hand

LOST

I lost my way, on a path overgrown.

With weeds of uncertainty and confusion.

Branches sway in the wind, whistling, enticing.

Voices, so many voices whispering.

Clouds form random shapes

In a grey sky that seems closer than normal;

Which way now?

A boy in a blue jacket walks by,

headphones feeding music into his ears as he strides.

With purpose, oblivious,

his dog running ahead; sniffing, tail wagging.

It pauses and stares at me before racing away.

Even to him I am insignificant.

My head spins like it does when I am drunk on gin.

I glance behind, dark shadows slide towards me.

A Darker Shade of Blue

Anxiety surging through my veins I stumble forward.

Dizzy with fear, a sense of dread creeping through

my bones.

Which way now?

I open my eyes, my arms like jelly.

Unable to lift the

duvet that has swallowed me up.

I close my eyes and whisper tomorrow; tomorrow I will get
out of bed.

By Mand Austen

STICKS AND STONES

Head down, she weaves between groups

of girls and wishes herself invisible.

They gossip about make up, last nights encounter

with the spotty ginger lad and geography homework.

Boys, dishevelled with grass stained shirts kick the stuffing

out of a football, their jackets in piles as substitute goal posts

Words like; 'beanpole' and 'freak' ring in her ears and tears escape

from her sunken eyes, that are underlined with dark semi circles

and etched into her pale face.

Sticks and stones, sticks and stones, she drowns out their

voices with the words her grandmother taught her.

A hole in the school fence enables her to wriggle

into a deserted playing field.

She throws her lunch away, a daily ritual, a comfort,

but her stomach rumbles in protest,

and remains empty once again.

She crouches hugging herself gently rocking,

willing the time to pass quicker.

Never had she looked forward to maths so much.

Her heart sinks as voices in the distance approach.

They swagger along, clad in designer leather jackets

and tight mini skirts, hair stiff with Ellnette spray

and blood red Rimmel lipstick;

giggling, preening, clouds of smoke encircling them.

The bell shrills and she dashes for the classroom.

The familiar words, 'weirdo' and 'loser' chase after her.

Sitting at her desk, numbers and symbols bounce off

the page, making no sense but it doesn't matter.

She looks at her watch, willing the hands to stop.

By Mand Austen

THAT GIRL WITH BPD

How much it effects me I wish people could see.

Emotions always spring up and down like high and low notes when you sing.

One minute you can take on the world no problem at all.

Then the next minute you're anxious to answer a simple call.

You're scared of what's to come.

It's drinking gambling to have fun.

People misunderstand think you have no feelings because of the stigma that flows.

When really you're just trying to get through the lows.

You care so much about everyone maybe and you're scared it's too much.

Everything can be intense from a relationship touch.

For me the self harm is compelling.

No I'm not a liar it's the truth I'm always telling.

People misunderstand people with BPD lie.

When everyday I'm trying to not let another piece of me die.

Sometimes you feel so broke you lie on the floor.

At my arms I claw one cut can turn extreme.

Your voices can become a team.

Don't tell me this is for nothing maybe I should see it as being unique.

But really it's help you should seek.

Because of them extreme emotions that can leave your body bruised.

These voices can turn your mind so confused.

Please don't judge me I wish to be just like you.

But there's no such thing as normal surely.

You can become poorly.

You need all the support you can get.

It can crush at all your nerves leaving you fragile.

It can leave you making suicide calls in a dial.

Help oh I'm small I'm lost how do I explain what's going on?

How a mood swing a high a low.

And the worst thing is it can leave you helpless; happening in seconds.

Some days you wonder if you'll make it through.

From season to season see the snow melt away.

Or if you'll even see the day.

Because you can't pull yourself out the sheets as the rain falls.

Pushing people away ignoring the cures.

I know it's not easy to trust.

Not when you're doing everything these voices are telling you.

Most demons controlling spiralling and you're just smiling.

But do you mean it?

I don't think you do but you'll do it anyway.

Where will you stay?

Feeling on top of the world or in bed.

What about them voices in your head.

How do you pull through why do these doubts exist?

I could write a list.

I'm stranded on an island stuck and put the heaviness aside.

Do I fight or flight or do I hide?

Sleepless nights growing cold.

What will my life be like when I grow old?

Emptiness rides.

My darkness hides.

By Natalie Hughes

YOU'RE NOT THE WINNER

Depression don't pretend to be in front.
You have not won so get the point.
I don't intend to waste everything god has given.
Because guess what I have an interest in livin'.
You've tried to win time and time again.
But I'm beating you with every line I write with this pen.
I'll say it again I have an interest in living my life.
One day I intend to be a mum and a wife.
You don't get the final say I do.
Although you've tried through and through.
Tried to strip everything away.
But guess what now I'm having my say.
Oh I swear I'll be strong.
You've controlled my life far too long.
You don't have my best interest.
You're a coward; a pest.
Trying to take all the good away.
Depression this is not your day.
It will never be your way ever.
You're cunning and clever.
However I just dodged your bullet.
You can't catch me I'm one step ahead.
I will welcome the day as I awake in my bed.
I will smile and live.
Because this life of mine has a lot of good to give.
Get my flow? I'm not feeling low.
No I'm on top of the world because I defeated you
depression.
Looks like I just taught you a lesson.
Now stay far far away don't come back.

No there's no loop hole.
I've retrieved the life you stole.

By Natalie Hughes

A WOMAN LIKE ME

You don't want to fall for a woman like me.

I have scars marked so deep that you can not see.

They are hidden away, buried beneath the skin.

How would I show you? Where would I begin?

Do I begin at the start? Back to my early years?

Do I begin by explaining? What's behind my tears?

Do I begin to uncover, each scar of the past?

Could I choke back my tears, long enough to last?

If I began at those early years, showed them first?

Would it be easier? As they were the worst.

Would those that followed, not be as difficult to show?

Would you still be the same? Even after you know?

Maybe after you've heard, being able to see.

You could understand the reasons why I'm just me.

You'd start to understand, why I appear to be cold.

Learning that each scar has its story, a secret untold.

Would you still want to look at me in the exact same way?

Would I still be as beautiful? As you saw me yesterday?

Do you still see a woman? That appears so strong?

Or a woman that's weak? After being strong for too long.

Then could you still fall for a woman like me?

If I was to bare my soul, for only you to see.

If I told you how my innocence, was taken away?

Stolen more than once, then would you still stay?

Could you still hold me? And never let me go?

As I shared the painful truth, about years long ago.

Days and then months, slowly turning into years.

When I lay there in silence, freeing the hardest tears.

Each night laying alone, my fear became my friend.

How long would it last? Would it ever end?

I was just a young girl. Laying frozen by fear.

Brown eyes tightly closed whenever I felt he was near.

I would force them closed, to pretend I was sleeping.

Laying like a statue, I felt my heart quicken its beating.

I'd let out a tear, for the sting to burn my cheeks.

Year after year passed by and this secret I did keep.

One that I had so deeply feared, so it went on untold.

It began at aged five and went on until turning twelve.

This age came with change, from a girl to young miss.

Even then, four years later, it never left my lips.

Years went on and I saw changes and I learned.

All things right and wrong, soon the tables had turned.

Twisting and turning, in time that table did fold.

It had left me broken, so my secret was told.

Word by word I spoke of the painful truth.

Of how a man I had trusted had stolen my youth.

I lost people that I loved, eventually my family fell apart.

Most looked away in disbelief, another scar etched on my heart.

This man was adored, even loved and respected.

He was battling an illness yet fought longer than I expected.

Each year he fought on, the more I had struggled to hide.

We were told only months but in years he fought five.

Retaining all of his dignity, it was too hard to bare.

He wasn't deserving after stealing mine all those years.

Why should I care? Or allow him that right?

Did he stop to care? When I had nightmares each night?

He had taken so many dreams, I was forced to see.

From an unfortunate age, how life is a harsh reality.

Behind closed doors after a truth was finally broken.

I appear to be grown yet inside I'm a girl still broken.

Broken by betrayal, emotional victim of pain.

I refused to allow 'victim', to be a part of my name.

Over time I found strength, in time I stood my ground.

I didn't prove my truth, eventually people came around.

With each year that passed I grew to be strong.

I stopped crying and forgave him because I wasn't in the wrong.

I have good days and bad days even the nights can be dark.

But I'm here and I survived; I'm a warrior at heart.

A warrior knows who to trust and who cares.

That's the reason that I am sharing my scars and my fears.

Since I heard, I felt the words that you speak.

Now with my scars, I give you my heart to keep.

My heart in your hands and the scars you will see.

Do you still want to fall for a woman like me?

Do you still want to be there from   my best days to my worst.

Now I've bared all of my soul and my deepest scar first?....

By Yvette Dove

sunshine

(Note: Author chooses not to use capitals in her work)

you were lost for so long

but i found you

i picked you up

i brushed you off

cleaned your wounds with daily love

watering you with positive affirmations

and look you're flowering

the sunshine in your smile has come home

and with that the storm behind those eyes

it's dissipating

sweet girl, believe things get better

you, yourself are proving it right now

there will always be rain and sometimes heavy storms

but you can always rely on the sunshine and rainbows that
follow

i know for a long time you will believe this was all your fault

question "why me?"

these questions i can't answer

i can't tell you that the triggers will vanish

i can't tell you that the nightmares and flashbacks won't sting

he may haunt your dreams

guard your past

but he has no grasp on your future

the sunshine has come home in you

you're safe.

By Natalie Male

stuck

stuck

can't move

don't want to

i want to stay safe in my sheets and never get out

i want to write poems

draw art

cook and colour

but with each passing moment

all i can hear is

the doubts and misleading messages

from the corners of my mind

telling me to do nothing

By Natalie Male

(Note: Author chooses not to use capitals in her work)

blackbird

14.18 glued to my chair

eye's fixed on my screen

case numbers are all i see

a blackbird

hey mr, how's your day going?

he looks at me for about 4 seconds before flying off

oh how i wish i could fly away

do you ever think about what it would be like to be a bird?

free to explore the world with a single spread of your wings

but yet

as i think harder about the life of a bird

or my friend mr blackbird

i can't help but feel slightly disheartened

they are alone

vulnerable and exposed

i realise that my friend

my blackbird

is as human as i am

no one is safe from this beautifully cruel world.

By Natalie Male

(Note: Author chooses not to use capitals in her work)

kitchen

the chaos that is my kitchen needs some attention,

like my mind

there is always some consistency of mess

the overwhelming amount of packaging

it's like i collect unnecessary things, like my head clogs up
with unnecessary thoughts

a sustainable level of bullshit clouding my worldview

my minds never silent

my kitchens never clean

By Natalie Male

(Note: Author chooses not to use capitals in her work)

speak

is it better to speak, or to die?

to speak

but speaking can be hard whether you are the speaker or the listener

it can ignite such conversation it would turn away even the most confident of souls

learning to speak to others and learning to speak to yourself are two very different lessons

i would say learning to speak to yourself.

honestly speak with yourself is a much harder journey

but the treasure you will one day receive has no competition

by Natalie Male

(Note: Author chooses not to use capitals in her work)

ASK MYSELF

I ask myself how can this be?

How did this happen to me?

The pattern repeats and life's too much

It wont be long till I lose touch

Mixed up feelings that rattle my brain

Do they understand all this pain?

Day by day it got brighter

All I hear, is you're a fighter

It'll crash and burn before my eyes

I'll stand there and tell you all the same lies

I'm okay, I swear to you

Each individual knows it's not true

I'll withdraw, sit and cry

Please I beg, let me lay down to die

Shan whats wrong? What can we do?

Let me ride it and hope I pull through

The guilt never ends

I constantly feel my life's a sick bend

It has to get better, it has to be brighter

I'm waiting for the day my mood is lighter

By Shannon Miles

WHAT IS THIS?

Have you ever been a soul alone?

You can feel it in every bone

The shaking hands

The shaking legs

What is this? You will hear me beg

The thoughts in mind

The most trying times

The tears they flow

Why wont they go?

The voices are loud

They shout and scream

You could only hope that you're in a dream

Skin is pale

Heart is frail

The pain you feel

It becomes surreal

You beg for a break before it's you

Clutching on please someone be true

You lie awake thinking of your past

Things that haunt you that never last

It gets better I heard day by day

Why don't you fuck off? Oh no please stay!

Racing thoughts

Lots of things bought

Energy rising but no motivation

My heads now like Grand Central Station

A simple task becomes so hard

My mind feels protected by a guard

You would think this was good

If only it were

I look around but only stare

What is this?

This hurt, this pain

No money will help

If only it would

It feels like a punishment for things I have not done

Someone pass me that loaded gun

Feel, hear and touch

All of this is far too much

Do not give up; I know you want to

Believe it or not this will help you in life

Open your eyes, you will see,

All of those who'll stand by me

What is this? Is it true..?

My darling, this is the making of you.

By Shannon Miles

THE BATTLE AT NIGHT

Let's lock up and go to bed

A little warm glow from what she said

But she's fast asleep before I get in

The little warm glow is turning dim.

My head has now started whirring

As you are laid next to me stirring

It isn't just once its happened before

Trying to stay calm with some light from the door

I don't want to be pathetic and weak

But I feel this way three times a week

I want to feel loved and emotionally strong

I used to be but what went wrong?

Anxiety is getting hold of me now

For better or worse it said it our vow

I want to wake you up to calm me down

But my weakness might be met with a frown

A Darker Shade of Blue

Negative things going around in my brain

Playing over and over till I'm in pain

Taking deep breaths to try and stay calm

I wish you were holding my palm

I'll be too worried tomorrow to give this a mention

All I needed was a bit of attention

Why didn't I wake you up?

Because it was only last week you wanted to break up.

Another negative thought and in kicks the brain

Everything starts going around again

By Anonymous

THE MORNING AFTER

As I wake up you're on your phone

You're so far away I feel alone

You get up and go for a shower

It's 7am and I'm already on low power

It's going to be another long day

I want to talk but don't know what to say

You go and dry your hair

Without a word like you just don't care

I need you more than ever

I am feeling miserable like the weather

Please come and show me some love

Give me some hope and we can rise above

You leave the house and get in your car

It's very early and work isn't that far

I lie in bed and try not to cry; You didn't even say good bye

By Anonymous

MENTAL HEALTH

Make sure you get the help and support

End of the day your mental health is important

Now there are people out there willing to help you

Time to get help and support you need

Appreciate there be those who are scared

Let's help thousands of people who need help

Helping those people with mental health

End the suffering of going through mental health issues on your own

Appreciate your mind

Let's help those people who look after our mental health

The time now to take care of your mental health

Here to help and support you with your mental health

By Jay Joshi

(note from author - I have felt my poetry writing has been a fantastic outlet for me)

VOICES IN MY HEAD

These voices in my head getting louder

The thoughts in my head getting worse

The pain in my heart getting stronger

And the only way I can let it out is words

You see the hidden pain is challenging

People can see it but don't know its strength

They brush it off and 'say you'll be fine'

But they don't know how it ends

You see not everyone is ignorant to your pain

Some just can't see how strong it truly is

You've gotten so good at hiding it

You can't understand it yourself

You look in a mirror and see a shadow

Of the person you used to be before

The shell of strength protecting you

Is crumbling with every thought

You've shielded yourself so good

But trapped yourself within

And now you realise that only words can help

But you can't understand how to begin

You see you don't know when the troubles started

Or how they came to begin

You tried so hard to fight them

You didn't see them come in

Knocking down your confidence and self-esteem

And now the only words you say to yourself

Are the words that are loud and mean

You see the voices in my head are so loud

The thoughts in my head getting worse

The pain in my heart is getting stronger

And I can't end this with words

The sufferings gone on too long

And I'm struggling to hold myself high

But please forgive me if I cannot say bye to the demon inside.

By Sammy Tharratt

HERE IN MY HEART

Here in my heart, and deep inside my brain
All I've got is heartache, bad thoughts and pain
I'm trying to make it better, keeping up my smile
But with all this suffering, it only lasts a while
I'm painting on a face, putting on an act
But this wall is crumbling, that's a likely fact
People just don't listen, or try and understand
I feel like sitting there and crying, it's getting out of hand
My brain is like a chamber just built for my suffering
Every word is torture, melting me to nothing
I wish I could escape this and be happy and free
I would do anything for me to just be me
But all I have at the moment is thoughts built to break me down
It's so difficult to keep this fake smile on and not frown
I need to start believing, I need to fill myself with hope
I need to stop listening to these bad thoughts, I need to learn to 'cope'
It's so easy for people to say this when they look at me
It's so easy "coz' they don't see the bad thoughts I see
I wish it was so easy, I wish I could be free
But I mainly wish for someone to see me for me

By Sammy Tharratt

THE SECRET OF SEA GLASS

Your entry into my life was not planned

Neither of us want to be here

This world has sharp corners

Corners that soft souls cannot fully command

I wish I could help you to smooth the edges

I dream one day you will lay a collection of sea glass on your window sill

Sharp edges weathered in your storm

Colours still glinting, a smooth reminder of your temptress.

By Leila Platt

PATIENT HUMANS

We are all human, we all have skin, bones and bodies,

But our frailest of organs you can not see with the naked eye.

You fill us with pills, white, blue, yellow and tell us we managed on them yesterday.

What has changed?

We make similar beeps as you when you test us with the obs machine,

But no one lays hands on the head that needs healing.

You, the ones, giving the pills, you have mental health too.

You become anxious when things 'don't go right',

Or maybe they just don't feel right.

In fact things that heal our bodies cannot always heal our minds.

Pills distort, dampen, punctuate days, demand compliance,

And dictate complacency in our management.

We seem cared for because we are given our pills,

Pills we don't choose because we don't have that knowledge.

Well I beg you to listen, you, the prescriber, do not have my knowledge either.

You see the colour red but is it the same as my colour red?

You may have seen and heard of deaths but not the same ones as me.

You eat foods, maybe the same as me, but what do you taste?

You have not tumbled down into the same hole that I try every day to climb out of.

If you did, you would realise I landed down here without a ladder or a map,

Then I hasten to suggest that you too would struggle.

What I need to do is write, explain, but the words in my head are a jumble.

Not smooth and deserving of crisp pages,

Angular and wearing like sharp edges.

We need green, the colour helps to calm they say,

But not if that is a tree falling on you,

And earthy colours,

But not if that is the soil smothering you.

I need to write and to talk and to tell my truth.

That truth may hurt, but it remains my truth.

By Leila Platt

LOCKDOWN 2020

It feels like a battle everyday,

As we tussle with news and other people's views.

More akin to a war or a wrestling match

Than an international healthcare emergency.

Whose voice do we listen to?

When it feels like those who lead us are unshackled?

We are left in the storm,

Some literally left out in the rain.

An international healthcare emergency.

Who's fighting for those who cannot?

Nothing about me without me

Constantly writing notes and doing your checks

Checking for what?

What I have, you cannot see.

I hazard a guess that I would not make sense

Of your scribbles, but they remain recorded.

Forever.

Yet it still stands

Nothing about me without me.

By Leila Platt

MID YEAR ENDINGS

It reached the time for me to leave

One ending is another beginning.

Even though I am going back to what I know,

Things still feel uncertain.

"You get to sleep in your own bed"

Is the common promise.

That bed was my prison some days,

Not too long ago.

I'd rather no bed than that prison again.

Time to focus on other new beginnings,

The garden, the green and the longest days of June.

The mid year ends, the mid year starts.

I carry on.

By Leila Platt

TURQUOISE GODDESS

Every day I look at you.

Your small but perfect form

Translucent in the morning light.

A turquoise pearl in my hand.

I'd like to make a necklace

Of you and your sisters.

But I take water

And swallow you instead.

By Leila Platt

DROWNING IN CUSTARD

Breakfast, Lunch, Tea and Supper

Eight, Twelve, Five and Nine.

Every day.

Porridge, Pie, Sandwich, Toast.

Puddings.

Drowning in custard.

Meals punctuate our hospital day,

Waiting to for what we will eat today,

And wondering what we might have tomorrow.

We can't cook, sometimes neither can they,

They have kind eyes behind the masks,

The people who serve meals.

So we eat, digest and thank.

Porridge,

Pie

Sandwich

Toast.

Would you like custard with that?

By Leila Platt

THE DOG IN THE FOG

Navigation through the foggy dew,

I nod in recognition to deja vu.

I know this intruder, what it puts me through,

My black dog nemesis, now in full view.

I stare in its eyes, there's no surprise,

When I need truth, it tells me lies.

If I don't fight, the bigger it gets,

A behemoth sized unwanted pet.

My senses numb as the fog draws in,

A regular visitor, I can't let win.

Emotions and thoughts are scattered, displaced,

Happiness and peace not easily traced.

A Darker Shade of Blue

Like Eleanor Rigby, I put on my mask,

I smile outwardly and stick to my task,

The black dog still walking by my side,

The fog still as thick, nowhere to hide.

But all things must pass, this I know well,

The dog becomes smaller, returns back to hell,

The fog vanishes one day when I awake,

A balance achieved, but it's only a break.

My dog in the fog will one day return,

With renewed torment and hate to burn.

His face appears with a knowing smile,

My lucifer hound will stay for a while.

By Mark Channell-Napier

RECOVERY

It was a cold and frosty day,

When I began to drift away.

Like the snowman melts in the glare,

I wanted to fade and lose every care.

I slowly put my head below,

I felt the water swirl and flow.

But through the haze I heard a voice,

Telling me I had a choice.

To continue on, with love and support,

Because to people, love I brought.

Times have been hard and the road has been long,

Sometimes I've felt like I couldn't go on.

A Darker Shade of Blue

I've had many a setback, failure and strife,

I've wondered what is the point of my life.

I overcame obstacles, chased my fears,

Gritted my teeth and smiled through the tears.

I began to see a glimmer of hope,

Those around me helped me to cope.

Now years have passed and times have changed,

I kept on moving through the pain.

I found the strength inside of me,

Enjoyment in helping others succeed.

Recovery is possible if you believe,

You can accomplish and you can achieve.

Like a star I shine in the dark,

I will be here to leave my mark.

Now I can see how far I've come,

As I turn to face the sun.

By Fiona Robertson

DIAGNOSIS

You stop, you look, you label me,

A diagnosis - that's all you see.

But I am so much more,

And I am the same person I was before.

I have talents and I have skills,

But you look at me and see my ills.

You laugh and joke about me,

You think I can't cope, but I don't agree.

For I am stronger than you know,

I will bloom and I will grow.

I've suffered hate and felt the pain,

My tears have fallen like the rain.

You made me feel worthless, pathetic and small,

When no-one was around to hear my call.

I've endured years of discrimination,

I've felt alone, in isolation.

I've been called every name under the sun,

To you it was a game, just a bit of fun.

Now times are changing,

Still, a long way to go.

People's eyes are opening,

Where once they were closed.

We are talking more than we ever did before,

But we need to carry on, we could all be doing more.

So, it's up to all of us to challenge discrimination,

So that we can become a kinder nation.

By Fiona Robertson

ADHD LABEL

Many thanks for my ADHD label, It fits just as fine as can be

It pulls all my names together and puts them where they ought to be,

You see Labels do all the explaining without them we only have names

And though names can give an idea it's clear they don't often explain.

Shy, lazy, messy, mad, wild and crazy are a few names I had for myself,

Generous, artistic, creative, unique, I was definitely like no one else.

Socially phobic, unorganised, disorganised with mood swings all over the place

Unstable, unable while missing my label, there's only one thing I could be?

I'd named myself stupid, 'SO STUPID' that used to be me

By Heather N

LIFE WITH BORDERLINE

I endured debilitating trauma

All I was left with was scars

And a personality disorder

Through the tears and the pain

I'm starting to learn to live again

Laughing with friends, loving family

And I'm starting to smile more slowly

By Ciara Perry

AND THE THOUGHTS BEGAN

And just like that,

The bad thoughts crept in

The flashbacks hit me like a bat

And I don't know if I'll ever win

By Ciara Perry

THE GIRL WHO HIDES

She has an empty stomach but a busy mind

An illness but not the usual kind

Having flashbacks, lots of tears

She sees some food but hides her fears

Calorie counting, tormented by the scales

Will she every be happy she wonders

As she looks into her every detail

By Ciara Perry

DARKER DAYS

And though the days get harder

And I can't think straight

The thoughts that surround me just won't wait

Pushing me slowly back down the black hole

Will I ever escape

That's what I want to know

By Ciara Perry

SABOTAGED

Did you know what you were doing

When you sabotaged my soul?

Constantly telling me you made my life

But it's not worth the one you stole.

You seemed good from the outside

But then again most people do

But I remember what was on the inside

Each little thing you put me through

You say 'it never happened'

Now I'm questioning my sanity

You made me apologise

Just to boost your vanity

By Ciara Perry

MANIA AND ME

We take it in turns. When it's madness's turn, I'm excluded.

I watch her snake in a figure of eight around the sitting-room

where she cannot sit, the dining-room where she cannot eat,

The stairs up-and-down-up-and-down – mania growing.

We take turns and for weeks she's combed this house

Fingers fidgeting each wall's small speck of dirt,

Bleach and cloth babbling over floors, skirting,

Blinding white paint until the entire house shrieks itself clean.

I ache because of her. She's a snow blizzard in July,

Starved, hot, living in the strip-light of her brain.

It flicks on when neither of us is looking

And its peeled-bright bulb pierces her skin

And she's dancing again in Technicolour.

I wait for her dying fall, the audit of medication,

The ration of too many pills in the house,

A Darker Shade of Blue

The lists-and-visits, list-and-visits, the waiting-rooms full of people sucking her air.

I sit with her in my body

The depths of her river a blood-orange streak through my veins.

I tell the doctor nothing has changed,

Adjust the clothing she's shifted.

Her underground railway pulsing under my shirt, down my legs.

And they can't stop moving

As if they're caught in water's pull, homesick for their body.

He tells me about time, as if it's running out.

And his old, grey face speaks of consequences.

She's joyriding inside me and I can't shut down her engine

And she's firing on all cylinders

And I'm the glass of the bulb at flash point,

That needs to be extinguished.

By Abegail Morley

STRESS

Stress. It's a funny little thing,

It's never just a single feeling.

It's a knot in the pit of your stomach,

A gliding plane ready to plummet.

It's jealously driving you mad,

It's creating memories you never had.

It's physical, emotional and mental,

It's a writing pad without its pencil.

Imagine a Robin singing in the trees,

A song designed and composed just for me.

Suddenly the singing stops,

You search every branch and rooftop.

Then you find that little bird who's lost his song,

Wondering where he belongs.

It's regret,

Finally understanding Romeo and Juliet.

Stress is denial,

Denying all thoughts have become suicidal.

Secrets and lies,

In the interest of loved ones, we deny.

Stress is heartache,

Knowing and accepting your inevitable fate.

A ticking tomb bomb of anxiety,

Is never accepted in society.

Love and support, we think we have none.

In this world, we believe we're alone.

Stress is a cult of survivors and warriors,

Some come home. Some stay at war.

Marching up the hill with "rifle and pack",

With one thing in common, our "plan of attack."

By Leah Jones

VOICELESS

The girl who always makes you laugh,

Cringes at the sight of her own photograph.

The one who calls you to check how you are,

For your wellbeing she'll go far.

The girl you vent your feelings to,

Inside she thinks "best you never knew".

Though none is through lack of trying,

You ignored her while she was crying.

Did you know she cries herself to sleep?

She's taken that heart off her sleeve.

Where? Where is her phone call?

Just 10 minutes. That's all.

A voiceless echo in the canyon,

Desperately searching for a companion.

You may preach and think you know,

She's never seen anything so faux.

Again, she turns the other cheek,

She'll never speak.

Though she tries with small success,

Before it's shot back down. Compress.

She listens to your endless worries and tribulations,

Lord knows she's had her share across the nation.

She won't tell you half of hers,

For the sake of not being heard.

You may call her your saving grace,

But can you see the pain in her face?

She hides it well, though its plain to see,

She's dying for a hero like you and me.

She runs and walks for charity,

You say you're proud with little clarity.

She prays for vision and acceptance,

As she marches on for Mental Health Awareness.

By   Leah Jones

BAD BRAIN DAY

Sluggish, slow

Unfocused fog

Plagued by the weight

Of the big black dog

Tired and numb

Everything a chore

Exhausted from fighting

This never ending war

Dark and miserable thoughts

Plague my mind

Yearning for comfort

And thoughts that are kind

Tears filling my eyes

Emotions astray

Battling on;

My bad brain day

By Stefanie Cantalapiedra

LITTLE LIGHT

Slither of light

Stand fast, stand bright

In pressing darkness

Stand firm, light the way

When all around is black as night

You shine like the day

Too easy can it fade to black

Forgetting what it's like to shine

All consuming, nowhere to turn

Forgetting how to be fine

You peak out from the shadows

Reminding me you're there

That little light of hope

In the darkness of despair

Don't let that light go out

A Darker Shade of Blue

Fight to keep it burning

There's more to life than darkness

The world will keep on turning

Fan the flames and feed the fire

Let it grow and flourish

Dispel the dark, fight off the night

Let it, your soul, nourish

Little light guide me through the night

Give me the courage and hope to fight

By Stefanie Cantalapiedra

LOST

It's better to have loved and lost than never loved at all?
This cliché only on the lips of those remaining tall
But we who stoop beneath the weight of someone we have
lost

Bent double by the crush of love we cry the tears of cost
The memory of a special smile once took my breath away
But now it takes me somewhere else beyond the light of
day

I follow you across the line where mortals never tread
And on the other side I walk pretending I am dead
Again we are together, all the wrongs are somehow right
For in this selfish deja-vu my heart can know some light

To be with you in fantasy is how I want to feel
It's how I stop the part of me that wants to make it real
I know my friends and family care, I see them through my
eyes

But deep within beyond their reach my spirit slowly dies
Oh sure I'll be ok in time and I'll find someone new
Another him, another her, but not another you

My heart is broken into dust and torment fills my sleep
Please let me choose the other path, this hill is much too
steep

For when it comes despair is yours and darkness fills your
soul

And living makes you wish to God you'd never loved at all
Yes we're all tough until it's us, we mock the life we live
We love like it will always last and take what others give

And thinking we are in control we watch our lives unfold
Each day a page is turned for us, our story slowly told
I stumble through each sentence, take the chapters page by
page

I play my part till evening comes then wander off the stage
Behind these eyes is where I hide, across the line with you
My body carry's on the show as all good actors do

It's better here within my shell where grief cannot survive
So understand this vacant frame and how I'm still alive
For in between reality and where I want to be
My shadow carry's on the life that once you shared with
me.

By David Foye

TRAPPED

Trapped in a prison of ugly thoughts
Crippled with anxiety
Slipping, drowning, so alone
Within society

Grappling with emotions
Smiling, struggling to cope
Yearning to shake this wicked skin
Recovery is the hope

Hating the mirrors reflection
Lacking confidence and pride
Each layer gradually peeled away
Striving, powerless to hide

The depression so exhausting
Persistent sadness and low moods
Isolated from the world
Fearing hostile attitudes

The panic attacks so sudden
Every episode is dreaded
Debilitating every time
The fear and stress embedded

Despair with every passing day
The anger so frustrating
Weary with the hopelessness
The thinking suffocating

The duty of care belongs to us
Being ones to lean against
To listen without judging
When worrying signs are sensed

Reaching out to those in need
When showing signs of grief
Lifts the burden like a laden weight
Bringing hope and much relief

Granting support and kindness
With love and humanity
Big shoulders taking up the strain
To act as therapy

Let's help our friends and neighbours
To assist the socially starved
Encourage them to share the load
Problems shared are problems halved

No one should suffer silently
So be there to take the call
From someone seeking solace
Mental health affects us all

In time, with lots of healing
This could become a memory
With hopes of a brighter future
To end the pain and misery

By Tina Patel

THE GOOD THE BAD AND THE MENTAL ILLNESS

Being in this place is fun sometimes: the stories.. the quirks.. the inappropriate jokes that only I hear.

Other times its nightmare.. a visual minefield, that I tried to forget exists, one no cliche aphorisms can soothe.

You can sleep but that only brings more darkness and passing of a man made illusion that serves as a biological clock

Dancing on the end of a pin in an attempt to sew yourself back together again

Other times you can hear the drop of a pin from self isolation

Times like that you have to make your own escape from this collagen fibre enclosure

That is meant to protect you.

Whilst doing something that's meant to better yourself, you might find a light-

like Christmas lights or the light of a light house guiding you away from the rocks.

It's beautiful but only exists in those minutes of wonder. Is that why my heart rate thuds faster?

It's beautiful but so alien and unexpected

The light is part of something a person said they loved about you.

They loved it so much they enclosed it in a box filled with pink love hearts that twinkle in the light.

Could that be my light?

By Shelley Pickles

TUNNEL AT THE END OF A TUNNEL

I can only see

Through the thicket of shrubs

A light at the beginning of the tunnel.

In front, there is a tunnel

At the end of the tunnel

I embark on this seemingly

Endless journey to freedom

Freedom from mental repression.

Looking backwards

Brings smiles

But the future

Is pregnant with frowns

Did I choose the wrong path?

Why am I alone?

Darkness eclipses my tired mind

A Darker Shade of Blue

And the strength to continue,

Flows out like endless rain

Sadly, there is a tunnel

At the end of the tunnel

By Elliot Misindo

THE SOLITARY MAN

The solitary man

Only lips seen moving

Up and down like drying leaves

Heart burdened and overloaded

With tears and grief

The grey hair tells the story

Of a thousand burdens.

Burdens older than his age

Sometimes music soothes

But never solves.

Strolling up and down

Without shoes

Everyone expects to see the pain

But it doesn't matter

Life has taken away

What it offered

What remains is the hope

To sail through these turbulent times

And somehow escape the billows

With the hope to mend

This broken vessel

Ravished by the storms

What else can one hold onto

Except knowing that every story has an ending?

By Elliot Misindo

PEACE

I long for peace

Peace flowing silently

Through my turbulent mind

To calm these nerves

Wrecked by depression,

Stress and anxiety.

To reorganise

This life which is a mess

Never a bed of roses

The once existing flowers

Have since wilted

Can you help me

Find the everlasting peace?

By Elliot Msindo

LONG DISTANCE JOURNEY

I'm at the beginning

Of this long distance journey

I embark

On this solitary journey

I get weary

And drag my feet

I get torn

And I pant because of the heat

Mind entangled by rushing thoughts

I should return

But on second thoughts

I should continue

I'm scared

But I'm not deterred

From going forward

Darkness soon returns

I should make the most of the light

And complete

The long distance journey

By Elliot Misindo

YOU'RE COMING

I saw you coming

With your lightning smile flashing

The rocky ride

You managed to guide

Your assuring voice

Left me with no choice

But to put my house in order

Is there still any disorder?

Your footsteps

Melted my fears

Stress has given me a fair share

But you have showed that you care

Problems came in series

But now you have left me with no worries

You hold my hand

Until the very end

By Elliot Misindo

DON'T LISTEN

Don't listen to the voices that fill your mind with dread

Listen to the voices that fill your heart instead.

Surrounded by the darkness it's easy to run and hide

Stand strong and keep on fighting then you can say "I tried"

When the exhaustion sets in and your world is full of pain

Remember you have been here before, stay strong and try again.

I want to give up.. I have had enough

My strength has gone away

I have fought and I have lost time and time again

But stand up and try again, maybe this time I will win

Being scared is not a good enough reason to ever, ever give in

I believe that no one loves me

That I am not worth their time

Repeated patterns of abuse has worn down my peace of mind

Find your strength, stand and fight,

Today you are not alone

Somewhere deep inside you know your fears are wrong

So don't listen to those voices that fill your mind with dread

Listen to the voices that love you and fill your heart instead

By Cira Hirst

WALKING IN THE RAIN

Walking in the rain, letting it flow over me.

Hoping it will wash away the sins that cling to me.

Will it make me clean?

Will I ever be clean?

Can I wipe away the pain as I swipe away the rain.

Drops fall in my eyes I am blinded by the hurt.

The pain so deep inside, ingrained into my very being.

Wishing that mother natures tears can wash away my pain.

Why does it hurt so much?

Longing for a human touch.

Yet never allowing anyone to get too close.

The rain slides down my face mingling with my tears.

How is it possible to have so many fears?

Scared to love, to be vulnerable, to allow myself to be laid bare.

People pass me by stopping my heart with their stares.

Please offer me a smile to brighten up my day and to let me that someone cares.

By Sarah Venamore

THE CHAINS ON MY MOOD SWING SNAPPED

You said you'd give it your best shot

But your gun wasn't even cocked

Now there's nothing: no compromise

Now there's nothing left inside

My regret I hold close to my soul

It's the only thing to make me whole

My mother raised a kid to stand on their own

Things are changing - I can't be alone

You don't fix the window, just replace the pane

But not pain is so deep it'll replace your face

How can I be so lost on the back of my hand?

This house, to me, is a foreign land

By Kiera Potter

FLY

Her soul is stained with your black ink,

These scars won't fade and haven't healed with time,

And still, she looks for a clearing

In this dark midnight sky,

Sometimes the smoke clears, and again it's back,

But one day, the tears will finally dry,

And she will see what love

Looks like for the first time.

You couldn't keep her in that cage,

You couldn't clip her wings and tell her lies,

You couldn't say fragile birds aren't meant to fly,

She wouldn't watch her life behind a rusty door

That was latched tight as her spirit slipped away.

All you could do was keep her in sight

Because beautiful creatures cannot be confined,

Her wings will grow and she'll find the sky.

By Kiera Potter

MY RIVER

One more screaming night

Puts the 'I' in fight

There's nowhere left to go

So I let my river flow

Down the mountain stream

Nightmares are all my dreams

Slammed the car door

I can't take anymore

Like a bullet in my eye

You never said goodbye

Tomorrow I'll fake a smile

Say it's alright for a while

Your childish ways failed

Your lies again unveiled

All happiness is lost

And it's all at your cost

You asked why I tried ending my life

When you act like my knife

One more screaming night

Puts the 'I' in fight

By   Kiera Potter

PROBLEMS DRY

Lay me down to sleep

Gin and tonic at my feet

A gun to the head

The only thing that could

Calm without worry

As my head becomes blurry

Grab your camera and shoot me

The only thing that could

You're my trigger, a loaded gun

Swallowing the bullets straight to my lungs

With every roll and hit I take

My lifeless mind will awake

I took the blade, a bottle, a noose

And then I snapped my mind in two

With the bottle and notion that I

Could drink my problems dry

By Kiera Potter

SOCIETY

In this mirror of society, I don't like who I see

I want to break free from Hell's agony

The poisoned truth, a painful lie

No one's there to see you cry

Make sure to choose your wear

Otherwise they'll laugh and stare

Choose your mask for the day

So you can be accepted in what they say

Look at the reflection, paint your face

Otherwise you're a complete disgrace

Brush your hair to perfection

So you won't feel rejection

Can't forget your perfect shoes

Looks like it's society to choose

Pretend to be happy and hide

Even though you're dying inside

Every word that they said

Infected this little girl's head

They dragged her down to the pits of Hell

Made her hate herself, but who could tell?

She was too ashamed to say a word

These photoshopped models she observed

Their pain caused her to turn to self hate

Maybe it really was too late.

By Kiera Potter

SUOIVBO SYAWLA T'NSI AIMILUB

She dreams of being model thin

Not realising she's bones and skin

Words of hate infect her head

Dreaming that she could drop dead

She somehow survives in her damaged brain

While still drowning in vomiting pain

Lies of insecurities flood her mind

Leaving her half dead and mentally blind

Living to hug her toilet side

Barely alive from purging her soul inside

Crying at her ugly reflection

She won't give in until she's perfection

She only eats numbers

Cries herself into slumbers

Even white roses have a black shadow

Still, no one can know

By Kiera Potter

TRY TO FLY

Try to fly with your wings of lead

Try to fly where they don't what you to go

It's easier to run; replace the pain with something numb

It's easier to go than to face this pain alone

The play filled lines from fingers to tips

You called me closer, a whisper to your lips

We danced the stage, spiralling down

They all cheered without a sound

I'm paying the cost, not getting the prize

Maybe it's time to grow wise

Go your way and I'll go mine

Are we really this hopeless against our time?

By Kiera Potter

GAD

What is this anxiety thing?

It is there whether the window

is open or closed, whether you

are early or late, whether I am

working or unemployed.

Whether I am asked to write a poem

or be silent, whether

I, we, you are living or not.

So I may as well write the poem

about GAD and send it,

whatever it does for my anxiety.

Whether there is water

or whether it is dry

God still loves me anxious or not.

By Matthew Rayner

UNTITLED

There is a war going on in my head, from when I rise to when I go to bed

To look at me you might not see, perhaps a glimpse is all there'll be

You might see me speak out loud, as if addressing a crowd

There is no one there though, away you will tip toe

I may appear distant and distracted, you speak and I never reacted

My eyes might dart around the room, and all you see is gloom

You give me something to do, yet I don't see it through

Your anger towards me begins to grow, then it starts to show

"What is wrong with you!?" is the common outburst, like a knife it pierces and hurts

I see the rage in your eye, in my soul I start to cry

At this moment I wish I could die

So, let me put the record straight, try and banish the hate

Within me something goes on, it doesn't always feel wrong

It is hard for me to say, even though I live with it day to day

"Please let them understand" I pray

I hear voices in my head or just over my shoulder, either outdoors or alone in bed

There, it is said.

Within is a quiet cacophony, a symphony of suffocating sounds

They threaten to surround and drown

Sometimes they're fun, I enjoy the company a ton

When they shout I want to flee, all they do is bring me to my knees

Some take the voice of relatives still alive, for their love is what I strive

Instead they cuss and criticise, cutting me down to size

Some take the voices of relatives now dead, They should comfort me when in bed

These fill me with the most dread, telling me I'm wrong in the head

Sometimes when it is too much I want to join them. Just be dead

On and on this criticism goes, it's relentless and never slows

I get up out of bed, immediately facing the dread

I go for a shower, there they wait to drain my power,

My confidence they scrub and scour

I go and get in my car, they tell me I will not make it very far

Whilst I try to work at my desk, they are there telling me I failed the test

Whilst I sit and eat my tea they are with me, "alone you will never be".

Then I try and go to bed, knowing tomorrow I'll face the dread

I don't want to leave this on a downer note, for those like me there is hope

When your head begins to ring, don't do a thing

Relax and picture a quiet stream, on the stream float leaves of green

The leaves are the voices, for them to affect you is made by your choices

Let them float away, to them no attention do you pay

Get on with your day

Speak to someone you trust, I feel this is a must

By all means show them these lines, I will charge no fines!

Do not think you are alone, help is always at the end of the phone

To the voices never give in, to do so would be the only sin

In the end when you are on the mend, the voices will change - love they will send

Nothing you have been through is pretend, you've just turned a bend

You are special, with this burden you might wrestle,

But you are the Captain of your vessel

If you bathe in your own self love, it gives the evil voices a shove

You have a great gift, it's only your perspective you need to shift

By Scott Jones

STEPPING INTO THE HEART

And so you stand in the furnace of your own heart

The ego deconstructed, taken apart

To build yourself up, years in the making

Now you feel alone and forsaken

The fire that once burnt so bright

Long since gave up the fight

You panic, 'How do I make this right!'

Your chest begins to feel so tight

This place, once the driving force for all your good

Now needs some fuel, anything! Coal or wood

Watched it go out, you did, as there you stood

Afraid to get your hands into the mud

Or to risk drawing your own blood

Where once you crafted your hopes and dreams

Now all that's left is a chapel to your screams

Again you look around

Listening for any sound

All you feel is that you've drowned

You can't hear the dream hammers pound

All that you were has been burnt to the ground

Then, you see it in your hand

The key to the salvation of this land

A flame that can be fanned?

You realise that all of this destruction

Was caused by an obstruction

The insight gives you the fight

Your hand now burns bright

To get back into the light

No longer must you fear your own might

In this might then, you realise

Without fear or surprise

Accepting of it, for you tell no lies

The obstruction was you

Search your heart now, you know it to be true.

So what should you do?

From out of the ashes of what you were, now rise

Cast off the ringing of your former cries

For in life there are no retries

Pick up now the hammer of your dreams

With its ringing you'll destroy the screams

Stand up tall, as a Phoenix in the fire

You're beautiful, reborn, for all to admire

Your spirit will not tire, no situation is too dire

Return to the forge, with its creations you will inspire

You walk now, proud and tall

Feet feel sturdy, you will not fall

To your own aid, you answer the call

As you stand before the cold forge, you do not stall

With vigour, you plunge in your power

This is your responsibility, you do not cower

This is your heart, your fort, your tower

The light from the fire bursts into life

Into the darkness it cuts like a knife

Through your own being it cuts like a scythe

And so you stand in the furnace of your own heart

A Darker Shade of Blue

The ego deconstructed, taken apart

To build yourself up, years in the making

Now you feel like life is yours for the taking

The fire that now burns so bright

Never truly lost the fight

You just had to make it right

You hold your hammer tight

This place, now the driving force for all your good

Powered now by your own self love, needs no coal or wood

Watch it burn brightly you do, now that you've understood

Off you go to get some mud

To forge your dreams, a promise to you bound in blood

Fear no longer cools you

Anxiety no longer suffocates you

Insecurities no longer drown

For you stand in the furnace of your own heart

Taking an active part

Ready for a new start

By Scott Jones

WHOSE LIFE IS IT?

Whose life is it? Is it mine? Is it theirs?

Whose life is it? As if anyone cares

Can you do this? Can you do that?

Make a cuppa, put out the cat

Ring the Optician, answer the phone

Take all the messages when I'm not at home

Do all the cleaning, iron the shirts

Make the dinner, vac the floor

That's your job, I do far more

You enjoy it, it's what you do

My works important, you haven't a clue

How tired I am and how stressed

A Darker Shade of Blue

Don't talk to me now I'm in need of a rest

My jobs important and one day you'll see

How I look after you so you look after me

If you do your own thing I cannot be sure

That I want you around and may show you the door

Because you know I'm important and one day you'll see

That your purpose in life is to look after me

By Hazel Boaler

CODEPENDENT

Who am I if I am not me?

When you look at me who do you see?

Am I no one until you make me someone?

The someone you want me to be

Look deeper, deeper you will find

I'm someone who has lost their mind

I gave it away when I ceased to be me

And became the someone you want me to be

By Hazel Boaler

NO MORE

I need to fight, I need to struggle

To have a life outside this bubble

To start to live more for myself

No longer living for everyone else

To accept that I, can take good care

And do not have myself to share

To find and keep good care of me

Then I will know who I can be

By Hazel Boaler

WHEN THE DAYS ARE DARK

When the days seem hard and there is no getting by,

The sky look glum and there is no where to turn,

You see your reflection in a shop window and you see yourself,

And think to yourself who is this person?

The person you see is not you.

As your heart beats as fast as as train

You start with this awful feeling of having no self beliefs

It starts from your brain making its way down to your feet

An almighty rush of dizziness overpowers your body

And you break down into an anxiety attack.

You try to fight it off but you can't,

People turn they eyes and stare

With a massive glare you become more unbearable

And you want to fall to the ground placing your head in between your knees

And you just want to hide

That moment you are all alone

And the world just feels far too big to share with others around

Time to run home to the comfort of being alone.

That you begin to calm, knowing you don't have to face the rest of the day.

By Emma Kirk

DEAR FRIENDS WITH ANXIETY

That feeling over you of impending doom,

The feeling of dread, the feeling of gloom.

It follows you round like a little black cloud,

You suffer the fears of getting stuck in a crowd.

Always a constant battle inside the mind,

Something you really struggle to leave behind.

Every morning you stand, and you put on your mask.

And you hide that you struggle with day to day tasks.

Upon your face you've planted a big fake smile,

And it's an extremely good one, you've practised a while.

You can feel so isolated and incredibly alone,

And you just can't shake it, like a dog with a bone.

But keep on fighting, and don't ever stop!

As that is the only way you can go from rock bottom to top.

Think of how successfully, these battles you hide.

And how many people are on the same ride?

Anxiety/Depression your cover is blown

I promise you friend, you are not on your own!

By   Natalie Robinson-Bramley

INSIDE AN ANXIOUS MIND

Sometimes in life you can get a little lost,

Sometimes you pay the ultimate cost.

Nothing's worth more than those who care,

The ones who love and with you they share.

Your blinded by the dark,

Your swimming from the shark,

The darkness follows you all of the way,

Until it's all night and there is no day.

But you see a glimmer, a tiny light

Chase it and don't stop til it shines bright.

Because when your dragged into that hole,

It's your self preservation it stole.

Only you can pull yourself back up again,

It's your mind, your body, your brain.

So believe that it will end no matter how gripping,

A Darker Shade of Blue

Lift up your head princess, your crown is slipping ...

By Natalie Robinson-Bramley

THE GIRL INSIDE THE GREY

She's the

girl who holds

her ears from the storm of

voices loud.

The girl to close her eyes

from the burn of sights

around.

The girl who cannot follow

every literal

word you say.

The girl you don't have

time to understand because

of her strange ways.

And

she's the girl you're letting

down

the girl inside the grey...

By Dawn Serbert

BETRAYED

Every single day

I feel as though I've been betrayed.

Not by other people

But my own infernal brain.

I know the words I want to say

I just can't get them out.

It makes me so frustrated

That I want to scream and shout.

I still recognise my loved ones

I recall all of their names.

But it's easy to confuse me

And I cannot be to blame.

You see I have dementia,

It's more common than you'd think.

A Darker Shade of Blue

I remember how to dress myself

And also how to drink.

I forget where I have left things,

It's not because I'm thick.

But Alzheimer's has claimed me

It's another of its tricks.

I used to be so useful

Now I feel no use at all.

A burden to my family

And I feel nothing at all.

My wife to me is just a friend,

My kids remain familiar.

My mental health is downgraded

Ever since I got dementia.

By Timothy Dutton

ELEPHANT

There's an elephant in the room

It appeared one night in the gloom

It grows every day

In a frightening way

While she beats it away with a broom

She's tried to brick it all in

But the mortar and plasters too thin

Now the rooms so much smaller

And the elephants taller

She's afraid she can't fit it all in

So what should the poor woman do

With a room full of pachyderm's poo

Is it time to move home

A Darker Shade of Blue

Like an old rolling stone

Or just move her chair into the loo

By Frank Chamberlain

ONE NIGHT

Your cry drags me from fitful sleep

3am, again

A hinterland time

There have been four interminable months of 3 am's

Bone weary, dreading what's ahead

A slender thread of hope, maybe it will be different this time

The weight of failure in every step I take to reach you

My aching arms pluck your wriggling, angry form from your cot

"Shhhhhhh. Mummy's here."

You feed greedily, content for a few precious moments

I sit rigid, my sore eyes blinking the seconds away until

You scream your despair, your disappointment

My throat full, I stop myself from doing the same

A Darker Shade of Blue

I clasp you to my shoulder, get to my feet and start the hours of pacing back and forth

Whispering into the darkness the words of love I long to feel

But my voice, my arms, my body cannot comfort you

I have no more to give

I sink to the floor, laying you in my lap

My tears fall and mingle with yours

Burdened with guilt

Bruised

Trapped in this never-ending ordeal

I'd dreamed of a bond of soothing satiny ribbon

Instead I'm bound by thick harsh ropes that chafe

Helpless, we struggle on as black night slips into grey dawn

Your accusing eyes hold mine

And like warring lovers we cry to each other

"Why don't you love me?"

Our answering cry

"But I do!"

Oh

The ropes begin to soften

Your protests quieten, you snuggle in to me

I take a deep breath, the first in months

I hold it, savour it

And I breathe out as you fall asleep in my arms

Dawn light blankets us

Hope surfaces.

By Wendy Janes

AN ILLUSION

We can't erase the memories of the son we knew before

Before paranoid schizophrenia came knocking at our door

He was full of fun and laughter he was intelligent and bright

We were totally oblivious to the years he'd have to fight

We've witnessed so much suffering loneliness and isolation

We were desperate for lessons in Psycho Education

We needed help to understand what you were going through

But no one thought to talk to us we didn't have a clue

Confused when you were seeing things distressed when you heard voices

Left out in the wilderness without support or choices

So confused when they said he's got a thought disorder

What the hell did that mean? So very out of order

As the years just came and went we needed a diagnosis

But for years it wasn't mentioned although we'd hear the word Psychosis

After 5 years I asked your nurse does my son have Schizophrenia?

You tell me was her curt reply now you must calm down Georgina!!!

Why no communication? creating years of sheer confusion

What is it about mental illness that makes it an illusion

By Georgina Wakefield

HOPE

Hope? it was lost – forgotten – hope? It scurried past us

Hope had slipped through our fingers the last threads lost in the vastness

Of the minefield that once was our feelings it got lost in a river of tears

Weighed down by the stress and the anguish of so many wasted years

Then just as we felt depleted we'd given up and could no longer cope

Like 2 long lost friends reunited – along came new found hope.

For 15 long painful years we witnessed your pain and isolation

Meer words are just not adequate to explain the loneliness the frustration

As years dragged by you survived without support from even one friend

Our hearts bled with compassion in this hell that had no end

Then we heard about personalisation it's aim? choice and control

Could it be this scheme could help you to reach just one meaningful goal?

Direct payments have made such a difference to your life and to ours

Places to go people to see no more long lonely hours

No more what can I do today? You could go to the drop in at Mind

Lost in a futile pointless existence in a world that seemed so unkind

Direct payments pays for a personal assistant she has also become you're best friend

Your quality of life improved no more sadness with no end

When you call and say I'm in London mum we've booked for a show and a meal

Hope shines through like a beacon light it highlights how I feel

So when you feel like giving up when you're thinking I just cannot cope

Remember - nothing is impossible and never lose sight of hope

By Georgina Wakefield

PSYCHI LANGUAGE

We were sent on a journey an emotional roller coaster ride

Like you we apprehensive like you we were petrified

We held on tight to the safety rail we faced the eye of the storm

We all had to learn a new language alienated from the norm

Clozapine Olanzapine Valium Prozac Sertraline

Anti psychotics make him robotic but life ain't but a dream

Lithium? - for moods swings - talking therapy

Counselling? - little impact – a longing to be free

A pat on the head and there you go son

Sit for hours at the drop in at MIND

Drugged up to the eyeballs with the liquid cosh life simply passing you by

Teams for every occasion no matter what's gone wrong

How are you feeling low today? Or do you feel you can't go on?

Psych nurses Social Workers OT'S with good intentions

Assertive outreach Crisis Resolution and Early Interventions

Silently screaming this life's a mess – does this one need to be assessed?

No real feelings anymore he doesn't even feel affection

Numbed by the monthly depots the inter muscular injection

Desperate Carers trying to cope hold on tight to a well weathered rope

Left out in the wilderness mum and dad are on medication

He cuts but we all bleed we feel his pain and his frustration

Schizophrenia has stolen our son but we do our best to carry on

Appointments with the DSS adds to our ongoing stress

Income support? - Incapacity? - DLA?

Which form plopped on our mat today?

Does he walk unaided? With a stick?

Is his heart beat slow or is it quick?

Can he boil and egg ? can he get to the loo?

How much does he rely on you?

We carers need them like the plague

We try to recall but the memories vague

End up in tears a blubbering mess – no thanks to the DSS

No improvement what's the answer a change of medication?

Hope renewed? No these new pills cause far too much sedation

What have we found the most painful dealing with this each day?

His young life simply passing him by? or watching his hair turning grey

When he was a child and he cut himself we could reach out for a bandage

But it's a very different story when you're forced to learn

PSYCHI LANGUAGE !!!

By Georgina Wakefield

SCHIZOPHRENIA? IS MERELY A WORD

Schizophrenia – there it's done

Schizophrenia ?– It's merely a word

But public misconceptions

Ensure that it's rarely heard

He suffers from his nerves we say

In hushed almost silent tones

Schizophrenia turns us into lepers

Sad subservient clones

A chicken and egg situation

Families scared to tell the truth

Even though our loved ones

Have lost out on their youth

Schizophrenia THERE – we said it!

We said it - now it's done

We refuse to hide in the shadows

Because we are proud of our son

Our dark cloaks have become too heavy

Were sick of standing alone in the crowd

We refuse to wear a meagre disguise

We intend to shout it out loud!!!

For the decades that it's been around

We've coped too well with ignorant views

We've thought of a new remedy though

Just try walking one day in his shoes

Schizophrenia is merely a word

And if we had our way

We'd shout it from the rooftops

Right here right now today!!!

In an ideal world we'd be teaching

Education is sorely needed in schools

Ensuring that new generations

Play hard and fast by the rules

We need them to see the difference

If this was cancer or sugar diabetes

The difference lies in respect

We can't afford to let this beat us

This is the age of technology

It's unbelievable disrespectful absurd

No more hiding in the shadows

Because - Schizophrenia is merely a word

By Georgina Wakefield

TODAY

Schizophrenia is merely a word

But it's a word that strikes fear in our hearts

It comes suddenly out of the blue

So bewildering right from the start

Like the huge waves of a tsunami

It swallows us up one by one

A huge ruthless soulless kidnapper

It steals our loved ones – daughters- sons

Schizophrenia shatters lives

Devastation lies in it's path

It tramples on our hopes and dreams

Like a monster that's fuelled with wrath

It's reputations made worse by the media

They poison vulnerable minds

With words like Psycho and Schitzo

Abusive disrespectful - unkind

What if this was someone they loved?

Perhaps then they'd consider our feelings

Would witnessing relentless suffering

Change their dirty dealings?

Schizophrenia is just a word

It's viewed as evil rather than sad

There's no thought for those who suffer

Or the lives that they once had

This is just one more tragic life event

The same as cancer or sugar diabetes

But these conditions are respected

We must never let this beat us

100 years it's been around or so the experts say

Schizophrenia is going nowhere

So we must change minds

By Georgina Wakefield

THIS ISN'T ME

The experts tell me I have complex PTSD

I don't want that diagnosis to define me

I am not a symptom of my past

Everyday I fight to create a fulfilling future where I will have a chance to make a happiness that will last

People often tell me that I am strong

They don't know the emptiness I feel inside or my desperate need to feel like I belong

All of my life I have felt out of place; like I am wrong

So many times, I have found myself sat on a swing alone in the dark singing the same old sad song

I have my emotions locked up tight, in a cage, afraid of what might happen if I allow myself to feel

I wake up each morning hoping it's not real

I have cut and burnt myself so many times just to feel like I am alive

Many nights I have dreamt, prayed, that I could just die

I look in the mirror and I don't recognise the person staring back at me

She looks worn, aged beyond her years

If you look closely enough you can see the stain of a million tears

This can't be me, ugly, fat, every inch a layer of the burden of my fears

I have refused to be a victim of my circumstance

I am so angry with myself for succumbing to this repetitive dance

Jumping at every sudden noise, easily startled like a deer caught in the headlights

Immediately reverting to fight or flight

I hate how this condition makes me feel

My heart pounding faster than a racing car wheel

Some days it feels like my skin is literally crawling and I scratch so much that my skin begins to bleed and peel

It takes such a long time to calm myself down and reassure myself that the danger is not real

Some days it feels like my body has been invaded by someone or something else

I am screaming at it to get out and pick on someone else

This isn't me, I am not weak and I don't want to appear like an animal's prey

I have made myself physically strong so I know I am capable of protecting myself and getting away

I have never had someone in my corner to protect me from the evil in this world

I had to learn this lesson the hard way when I was just a little girl

The therapist tells me I need to learn to trust someone and let them help me

It's easier said than done when I have had no-one to support me.

I fear I will spend the rest of my life alone because that's the only way I can feel secure

Too many people, close to me, have hurt me so bad it's left me feeling unsure

I no longer know who I can trust, not even myself, and I'm afraid that this feeling will never be cured

I just need to keep looking in the right direction and hope my inner strength will help me to endure.

By Katie Westlake - "Complex PTSD sufferer"

CHROHNIE

I was a frosted flower exposed to light; x-rays, MRI's or pure sunlight?

I suck on snowflakes rather than dew for mere sustenance.

Survival

Why survival?

Injections, needles infusions, appointments, hospitals, antibiotics, assessments, herbal remedies, yoga, inner peace, inner peace, inner peace, brain scans and body scans and new treatments and old promises

Shocked faces gripping clipboards and strained smiles clinging to a normality and weeping for my normal nightmares

I'm a struggling, struggling refugee soul and all the strangers know.

Strained smiles, shocked faces and bloody places

A sad little creature, burrowed deep inside, stares at me

Screaming why?!

I cannot answer her screams for they are another me and this silence this silence surrounding me is so, so sweet

The metal in my back is cold as I'm spread out like a slab
of meat

My hair is sprawled out like a broken halo

Death brushes my lips with a bittersweet kiss, teasing me
with his knowledge

and dropping me back into a fiery twist

A hell with no end, with tastes of heaven in between,
survival

Why survival?

I'm diseased, not dead

I'm diseased

Not dead

Salvation lies in me and not in a stranger's smile

Snowflakes tumble upward and I am free, free to fall

This is what after means

but what comes next?

By Sarah Fox

DEPRESSION

Stealthily in dark corners of the heart,

is settling a germ plasm of despair ,

nurtured in silence,

suffering by guilt,

Ridiculed beyond measures

Joys of life in fading spectrum

Shades of grey covering glee

Every passing day

Pushes life towards circles dark

All emotions in negative shades

Urge to cocoon

Thrust to end

The victim walks on

A diminishing thread

the tight lips,

the lone shudders,

Doors of loneliness

Bolted strong

A friend

A guide

A mentor

Has to knock

Break the ice

let's talk,

let's shoulder the burdened soul

Push the button

Erupt the volcano

Allow the lava to flow

Burn the negativity to ashes

Bring back life

On autumnal branches

Help them again to grow...

@ 'dusk'……

By Bipul Banerjee

UNSPOKEN

You hide your pain in a smile.

No one needs to know

of the pain and hurt you feel inside.

It's yours and yours alone.

You drag yourself out of bed,

through the tears and the pain.

To see the sun come up again,

is another day darkness did not gain.

But those days get less and less

as you withdraw from the world.

An empty shell of what you were.

Just misery in which you swirl.

A Darker Shade of Blue

Your smile no longer showing

You spiral down and down

But there's always help at hand

From everyone around.

They pick you up when you're not strong.

They're a rock when you are not.

Open up and let them in

before you lose the plot.

Depression, it's a killer;

People hide it out of sight.

To break the taboo of this disease

we must stand up and fight

By L.W.Rogers

HE CRUMBLED

He crumbled before me

No warning

No signs

Just a broken man

Who needed fixing

Who needed repairing

It took time

It took patience

It took medication

It took a range of health professionals

To fix him

To patch him up

To monitor him

To make him who he was again

I know what I lost

I know what I gained.

By Kauser Parveen

SHOUTS IN WHISPERS

She shouts in whispers

Into my ear

I am the only one

That can hear her

I am the only one

That listens

She shouts in whispers

To be heard

To add strength to her voice

Her shouts make her feel

Present

Empowered

A contributor to the bigger conversation

A conversation about her

But not without her.

By Kauser Parveen

I CAME HERE

I came here

To talk

Talk through my deep dark

Thoughts

Talk through my deep dark

Suicidal thougths

You sit across me

Offer me words of comfort

Words of encouragement

You offer me space

Allow me to be a child

Explore

Paint, draw, colour a world

I can draw

The life I have

The life I want

Bridges the gap

Of the journey that is needed

By Kauser Parveen

DARE I SUFFER ALONE

Dare I suffer alone

In a mind that stays the course

In a life that speaks to the world

In a dream that shows all the rain

Dare I suffer alone

Among those who suffer around me

By Clive Culverhouse

MY WALLS

These walls are my sanctuary

guarding me, looking after me

stopping me, restraining me

my prison but my safety

where I hide

where I rule

a brick cloak of invisibility

You can't come in unless I let you in

I'm the master here

the prisoner here

the one who is suffering here

the one who is surviving here

A barrier, a security

my light house, my castle keep

an obstacle, a safety net

These are my walls

where I live

where I stay

Within these walls I'm stopping here

By Clive Culverhouse

LOST

Wrote it out and letters flowed

Under a shelf the crows did crow,

By the lamp in the corner of the room

The plug sockets begin to whisper of doom.

The kitchen sink had been overthrown

The tap had decided on an absolute no

The plasterboard cursed and swore

As the carpets crawled across the floor

The lightbulb had committed suicide

The mirror disgusted, could not abide

The cd's decided war to be made

The dvd's had tried to invade

The wok was angry nothing was made.

The milk was off but still in date

The cheese had crept

Grown hairy and wet

The candle sang a sweet pure glow

The coffee table enjoyed the tiny solo

The couch sighed deep

The shoes prayed for feet

The saving foam lay quiet and wept

The razor blades denied regret

The freezer buzzed with cheep delight

The candles lost the ability of sight

The radiators were sly with cold

The tins of soup felt wrinkled and old

The wooden spoon was burned then sold

A new black sock went grey with shock the skirting boards
pointed and mocked

As a toothbrush choked twisted and coughed

The eggs were angry

The spoons were not

And when it hit twelve

A Darker Shade of Blue

The clock just stopped.

By L.S.Parsley

WHO AM I?

Who am I you may well ask?

I wish I knew, then it could be true

I am the girl who appears normal but feels abnormal within

Feeling different, feeling like I don't fit in

I am the girl who feels misplaced,

like an alien from outer space

I am the girl with the racing mind

always overthinking, always seeking explanations for it all to make sense

oversharing to offload then beating myself up for what I have told

I am the girl who worries what people think,

replaying everything that I speak, thinking they must think I'm a freak

I am the girl who is matter of fact, finding these unspoken rules harder to grasp,

Inconsiderate some may say, if only they could see it my way

I am the girl who is kind but naive,

the observer of the good, and blind to the bad

the gullible character that falls for the act

I am the girl who finds socialising so fun and laughing at a good pun, feeling of togetherness the awkwardness subsides

I am the girl who likes to do things alone,

some thinks I'm odd, some says I'm brave too much social overload just pickles my brain causing my battery to drain,

I am the girl who obsesses and collects, does everything to excess

There is no in-between, moderation and me just do not agree

I am the girl who was once lost but now I am found,

years of wondering why I am, the way that I and now it's so clear its profound

Now I can accept who I am and be content with being just me

So, who I am you may ask?

I am a girl on a journey of growth, both learning and accepting me as I am, I may be different but I am exactly who god made me to be, I have a purpose I am not worthless

I am Claire and I'm finally happy with just being me.

By Claire Arnold

"Im 26 years old and I recently got diagnosed with aspbergers . All my life I felt different , felt like I didn't fit in . Also I had such bad depression It got to the point where I tried to end my life. I have cam through the dark times now and turned it around , I finally feel whole and I accept myself for who I am , I'm the happiest iv ever been. I wrote this poem to hopefully help other people in a similar situation".

THE TUNNEL

Trapped, alone in an endless tunnel,

The low light fades with each step taken,

And the long path behind crumbles and falls.

The cold sinks down, in through the slimy brick walls

And chills the bones from the inside out and

Sets the constant shivering in motion.

As each moment passes by unwanted,

The search for an ending or at least a light

Grows more desperate and less hopeful.

Then it appears -

A glimmer, amidst a wave of relief,

As if the mind plays a trick on the soul.

But then it morphs to a blinding holy light

That stings weary and broken eyes red-raw

Singing sweetly of a promised freedom

Salvation: The final hope of a way out,

Hides itself out of wicked cruelty

In front of a speeding train.

By Holly Nesbitt

THREE VOICES, ONE WHISPER

Within two weeks, three of my closest friends whispered to me

That they were on anti-depressants.

Discretely – as if this secret we now shared

Didn't deserve the vibrations of a murmur,

Let alone a voice.

And it took me until friend three to pay attention

To this gross imposed discretion

They all felt they had to mention:

'Don't tell the others,

please'

'don't say any

thing'

'is, I don't want people to know.'

Their three voices were one whisper.

Quietly lonely.

And if only I hadn't promised to

hold my tongue,

I'd have told each of the three

about the other two,

And then maybe they'd have felt

more than the only one.

By Beth O'Brien

CONFIDANT

I give other people the advice I tell myself,

And ignore,

Hoping they won't do the same.

I tell them to take a break before they burn out

When I've had four hours sleep.

I say that skipping lunch is awful and won't help,

Then nearly do the same.

I assure them that sharing their problems

Isn't burdening anyone,

But then won't share mine when I know they have

Their own shit to deal with.

In short - I'm a hypocrite - the personification of

Do as I say and not as I do

By Beth O'Brien

I FEEL LIKE I HAVEN'T EARNED IT

Was how I first put into words

Why I wasn't eating.

My morning routine involved a 30 minute run

before I skipped breakfast.

I drank water all day long so that

I felt like I was full,

And maybe I'd have a coffee because

Liquid didn't count.

I'd study until it was time

To skip lunch too.

At home, I ate dinner because

They'd notice if I didn't.

But eating felt like failing – the thing I was

most scared of – So

I'd be sick to repair the damage my

broken will had eaten.

It felt easy - or -

seemed it at a time when

nothing else did.

By Beth O'Brien

BREATHING

I sit with the window open

(even though it's freezing)

Because it reminds me that

I have to keep breathing.

Shivering keeps me moving

(so I know I am not still)

Icy air sears my lungs

(so I know they haven't

stopped

By Beth O'Brien

DARK RED DAYS

Ruby warm trail

Trickles from my wrist

Splashing on the floor

Crimson drip

Crimson drop

Slashing slicing

cutting my desolation

Painful torment…

glimpsing reprieve

Past the point of

Inner death

I exist in an after-life

By Jacqueline Robinson

MISERY

Misery

Despair flicks the switch

Turning off hope

My should melts like wax

Liquid thoughts slip away

Desperate tears bring no solution

No one hears my shouts for help

They hand silently

In the air

I'm trapped

What's the point of living when I have no hope?

I plead with family for help

They don't see me

I'm masked by a shroud

There's only one way out

As love cannot

Keep me in this world

I sit alone

With the noose of loneliness

Around my neck

Although I'm physically alive

I'm dead inside

Withered and decomposed

Facing no future

I may as well

A Darker Shade of Blue

Bring it all to a close

By Jacqueline Robinson

2 pm APPOINTMENT

Holding a fingertip to his right ear;

this is the worst part of the memory:

all bright, vivid. He is still forced to see

and feel the machete: cold steel, cold fear.

Now he dreams, cannot sleep, was driven here

by his wife. Four or five men, he tells me,

balaclavas, jumped from a van. Now he

lies with a blanket of guilt, but it's clear

to me that he wants to become the man

that he was. That he did the best he could.

As you've come through pain and grief in the past,

you can do that again. Sounds and sights can

go. We'll create your Safe Place now. I'll put

you in for next week. This stuff will go, fast.

By Fokkina McDonnell

Note: this sonnet is about EMDR (Eye Movement Desensitisation and Reprocessing)- a proven trauma treatment which has been NICE-recommended since 2005.

OUTSIDE IS NOT FOR OUTSIDERS

Outside is no place for an outsider

Best stay inside where they leave you alone

Outside love and friendliness is not condoned

Especially for those who are not of this zone

Out there they just stare at one who is not their own

Beware of the outside when you're an outsider

What might happen to you out-there is unknown

Inside is far safer than outside for an outsider

Outsider, you'll never hear, "Hi, Hello, or Shalom"

'Lonely,' is the name of this city they call their home

A Darker Shade of Blue

So, outsider, best heed my sincere reminder

Don't go outside when you an outsider

Stay inside, be content with being on your own

By Kim Solem

Dedicated to those who suffer from agoraphobia.

MUROIDEA PARANOIA

Like Lucifer's fall from grace
I dropped from the human race

Neurotic paranoid schizoaffective with addiction
Into the dark I retreated with my mental affliction
Dilapidating in desperation I prowl and sneak
Nearsightedly on hands and knees I rummage slink and creep
Scavenging the sewers, gutters, dumpsters, clutter and alleys
Of garbage and sewage for digestible grubbery
Filthy frizzled frazzled mangy hair crawling with lice and fleas
My surviving mustard-coloured teeth decay with disease
Like tusks over my withered lips only a few remain
My dirty untrimmed fingernails are yellow and frayed
I'm harmless, yet people are startled at my sight
So I prowl in the lonely shadows of the night
My humanity is slowly disintegrating
Tweaking ticking twitching scratching shivering
Body constantly moving in psychomotor agitation
Chemical mortification of the flesh in declination
Some dumpsters are better than others
Some swill and garbage has more to offer
My infla me to a steel cornucopia of bakery leavings
Where I feast on musty maggot-infested sweet breads
With such abandon I'm oblivious to the iron jaws of death

"Hey Jack…Jack!
Come here quick!
Look at the huge rat
I caught in my trap!"

By Kim Solem

NOTE FROM THE AUTHOR: Diagnosed with cancer can be a humbling experience. Though I never had a substance abuse problem, the synthetic opiates I took, along with the effects of chemo, were devastating to my psyche. I suffered terribly from depression and paranoia. Plagued with insomnia, I'd wander the streets at night. I looked like a wreck. My hair fell out in patches. Due to acute dry mouth, my teeth literally rotted out of my mouth. People avoided me like the plague. I never felt so alone. For the first time in my life, I identified with society's outcasts. One night, I had a horrible nightmare that I was trapped in a dumpster crawling with rats. I awoke drenched in sweat and trembling in fear. This poem is a dramatic reflection of those very dark days.

AGORAPHOBIA

Fearful anxiety

Exaggerated nervousness

Social psychosis

Incarcerated at home

My inescapable prison

By Kim Solem

SCHIZOPHRENIA

Mental disorder

Schizoaffective dementia

Hallucinations

Psychogenic confusion

Intellectually tortured

By Kim Solem

PYROMANIA

Blazing obsession

Incandescent enchantment

The allure of fire

Sets my intellect ablaze

With flaming fascination

By Kim Solem

INSOMNIA

Insomnia's song

Irritates all through the night

Without lullabies

If only I could sleep a wink

In the morning I could think

By Kim Solem

BULIMIA NERVOSA

Eating disorder

Insatiable appetite

Binging then purging

Gastronomically cursed

Merry-go-round in reverse

By Kim Solem

LITTLE STOP SIGNS

In recent weeks my body has been pleading,

I've never had hay fever or weak legs,

But my eyes burn unexpectedly in the night

as if the dark is something else, a blanket of hessian

Drawn tight beneath my eyelids.

And so I shuffle,

Rag doll, rough cloth eyes,

Limbs creaking in brittle pain like overbaked gingerbread,

Crumbling too much to build a house.

And my skin.

There's only so much I can cover.

The bruise-shade slack beneath my eyes,

Taught blistered palms and

little warning signs

up and down my arms, my legs, my chest,

Which say STOP.

Drink more water, get more sleep, do a rain dance, bloody do something,

we're failing here.

By Isabelle Evans

TRAUMA

A glass shatters,

You try to mend it,

Stick it back together to function as it

once did.

How do you stick IOOO fragments back together?

Eventually, with the help of glue,

We have something resembling the glass it was - once upon a time.

But it was so violently shattered, shards are missing.

It is no longer functional.

By Deb Shaw

WINTER OF THE SOUL

My soul resides in winter,

In a land of leaden skies, devoid of any colour.

My soul resides in winter,

Freezing rain slashes my being.

My soul resides in winter,

In a barren land desolate and cold.

My soul resides in winter,

No sunlight sparkles on aqua seas or dances on emerald leaves.

My soul resides in winter,

Eternally waiting for summer.

By Deb Shaw

MY FEELINGS AND STRUGGLES

My feeling of lonely is not really new

I've had it for years not just a few.

I'm constantly anxious but try not to show,

That's a sign of weakness I tell myself so.

My body it aches and my brain it is fried,

When it all started a piece of me died.

I've hid it for ages, nobody knows,

That each day goes by the loneliness grows.

There's time I seem fine to the people around,

But trust me I'm not, inside pain does pound.

The feeling of sadness, worry and hiding this ghost,

Is the things that bring on the stress the most.

That tightness of stress that surrounds my torso,

I try to deter but it tightens it more so.

I feel like I'm locked in a constant fight,

A Darker Shade of Blue

My thoughts are killing me all day and night.

I'm recently married-i should be delighted,

I love her, I DO , but still my head's blighted.

I'm fearful of these feelings ruining our plan,

I want to be a dad and her a great mam.

But the more this goes on the harder it is,

I want to reach out but do the people exist.

I've talked to doctors and they give you some pills,

But what does that do for an issue like this.

I don't want to worry her or anyone else,

But my life has turned into a living hell.

I want to defeat this but don't think I can,

I haven't the energy and feel less of a man.

I feel ashamed, why can't I be fine,

But I just can't rid these demons of mine.

I can't see a future without these dark days,

And I'm pushing the ones that are closest away.

A Darker Shade of Blue

I want to scream and let it all out,

But I don't have the balls to make that shout.

I would end it tomorrow if I didn't have her,

What kills me is she deserves so much better.

This is a cry for help, but just for my reading,

By Ciaran Byrne

note by author: Please get the help you are needing

A BLUE DAY

No light wakes me today

and the sun's still asleep.

The darkness of my heart smothers the light

and stifles out every drop of brightness.

I can't get out of bed this morning

because my body aches and I don't have the strength.

I don't think I'll open the curtains just now

in case the light comes in and hurts my eyes.

I'm just slow to get started this morning.

I want to wrap the covers tight around me.

I press my face hard against the pillow.

I've got a headache again.

I roll over in bed and look at the alarm.

Time moves too slow right now.

I feel like I'm trapped in a hell dimension,

in a bad place, I'll never escape from.

The world's dark and sharp all around me.

I feel knives stab into my skin.

The dark rivers of my heart run cold.

There's no heat to light up the inside of me.

By Pamela Scott

BLUE-EYED GIRL

heavy head, unseen weight

pinning her down, stiff limbs, like

blocks of cement, stone

she can't breathe, trapped in

thick tar, suffocating, claw

at her throat, panic

sadness in her heart,

tears fall in the dark, light hurts her

deathly pale skin, leave scars

By Pamela Scott

HOW MANY TIMES DID I CRY TODAY?

The first tears fall

when I have a stupid

argument with my lover.

 An innocent remark,

misinterpreted. I find

myself sniping,

quick to anger & tears.

 The second tears

come when I'm

finally told, after

two weeks that

I didn't get a job

I interviewed for,

that I really wanted.

 I feel tears of frustration;

anger,

self-pity,

disappointment,

resignation

and defeat.

 The third tears

fall, unexpectedly

in the toilets.

I'm not thinking or

feeling anything

in particular.

 A wave of

sadness sweeps

over me, so

intense it stops

my breath. I

feel my face

fall apart

and the sobs

shake me.

 I cry like

a child

and cover my

face with

both hands.

My mouth trembles,

the sadness fills

every inch of me.

 I'm on

the verge

of tears all

day, sorrow

simmers below

the surface.

 I just want to

lie in a dark

room, hug myself

and rock.

And I don't even know why.

By Pamela Scott

TO GIVE A THING A NAME

I've always felt this way:

up and down, intense,

moving from one extreme

emotion to another,

bursting into tears for

nothing, quick to anger

and quick to tears.

I never knew not everyone

felt this way.

I never knew there

was a word for this

D E P R E S S I O N

By Pamela Scott

YOUR MIND IS NOT YOUR OWN

Your head

does not belong

to you. Not

necessary to anyone

else either.

Every

day is hard,

full of bricks,

stones and broken

glass, making neat

little cuts in

your most fragile

parts.

Your head

is full of

nasty thoughts that

want to hurt

you.

Different voices

that are part

of you, argue,

shout and spit

at each other.

You swear you

can feel blood

drip from your

ears.

You wake

in the middle

of the night,

A Darker Shade of Blue

crying like a

baby, snot running

down your face.

You don't even

know why you're

so upset.

You

just know your

mind is not your

own, has been

hijacked by the

blue hearted brigade.

By Pamela Scott

AFTER THE DARKNESS

It's when I wake and realise

I feel happy today

that I know the cloud has lifted

and everything is exciting and new.

I no longer have to force a smile,

say I'm fine when I'm not,

drag myself through the day

on the cusp of tiredness and tears.

Pleasure returns to the things I enjoy,

and light overcomes the darkness,

nothing has changed yet everything has.

I have my life back; I'm in the world.

By Heather Walker

BLACK DOG

He sees things only in black,

I want to colour his world,

offer small windows in sunlight

but he shuts the door on me.

He can't tell me why or what,

I can't tell him when it will stop,

only that it will. I rock him,

my baby in men's clothing.

Later, when I'm alone I cry

my helpless heart out,

wishing I could turn his negatives

to positives and magic away his pain.

By Heather Walker

WHAT MY BEST FRIEND DOES AT NIGHT

There's strength in routine

A cut tight habit

Even your wounds are symmetrical

Your own little joke

Straight red scratch lines

Line your long limbs

like an okapi's white stripes

Your photographic memory

 makes me know that you see her

lying there in a hospital bed

Every time

You try to capture feeling

in a blade's edge

A controlled madness

Pain with precision

You line your arms and legs

Section by section

Until they section you

You want to hide hard enough

that they let you go

This new end to an old routine

This is what my best friend does at night.

By Zoe Alford

THE ART OF WINNING

The art of winning can be hard to master,

when struggling with your own internal fight,

first a storm then sun and rainbows after.

If only tears of pain were tears of laughter,

confusion means you don't know left from right,

and makes the art of winning hard to master.

The smallest problem feels like a disaster,

when darkness calls and steals away your light,

first a storm then sun and rainbows after.

Grey skies are sunless, cheerless and just a

shade of black, they are not a shade of white,

and make the art of winning hard to master.

A Darker Shade of Blue

You can't slow time or get it running faster,

night follows day, and day will follow night,

first a storm then sun and rainbows after.

Fallen birds and angels always cast a

shadow, from ashes a phoenix takes to flight.

The art of winning can be hard to master,

first a storm then sun and rainbows after.

By Gill Hawkins

THE BLACK

Susie blossoms with black eyes

beneath a darkened, cloud filled sky,

wind snatch, black umbrella's broken,

exposed then Susie gets a soaking.

Back home, black mood, black thunderclap,

her black cat drops onto her lap,

demands her time, all her attention

and fills her with more apprehension.

A power out within the mind,

the shutters down, a black out blind,

locked in a room, trapped with her fate

from which she'll never quite escape.

At times like these she just can't cope,

there's no sense of anything, no hope,

for admitting black maligns the name

and things will never be the same.

She fights to keep the beast at bay,

ignores the slights that come her way,

as she suffers at the unkind hands

of those who'll never understand.

By Gill Hawkins

BELIEVE

How can I stop all your pain?

Try to teach you to be strong.

When are you going to see,

That is the world who has it wrong?

You have a beautiful soul,

And you need to understand,

That we shouldn't change ourselves,

Not for love, not for friendship, not for anyone.

I want to give you my strength

The understanding to carry on,

So you can believe

That pain can move on.

I hate to see you cry,

For things out of my control.

I wish I could put into words,

And make you see,

That is the world who has it wrong.

By Cassandra Neves

GOODNIGHT

it's not nice anymore.

it's a mess

an unmonitored mess

why won't someone fix it?

the books say one step at a time

one step in front of another

one moment out of time

to mark

to shatter

to disentangle

to disentangle the soul

from the person

the pathetic person

the pathetic little person

me

to disentangle me

little, pathetic me

i need detangling

detangle my head from my soul

my brain from my heart

the arms

the waving, stuffed arms of death

that grace the presence in A Room of Importance.

Too important for you.

Too important for me.

Inconsequential.

Until your arms are stuffed?

Gracing your presence in the room of death...

Chaos

you don't matter

you are matter

matter of no consequence.

Flip the switch.

By Nicola Smith

FOCUS PLEASE

She sits there telling me about

Her day.

What she does,

Where she went.

I don't understand visions

Appear.

She's dressed in

A white dress.

Who's the young chap standing

By her?

Wearing a suit with a white

Carnation in the button hole.

How come we are so old

Now?

People say, "Lettie has become

Nurse, mother and wife".

By Christine Law

GAME SET AND WIN

Every thing is laid out upon the

Table.

Rosie my life coach sits down

Opposite.

She is very kind and patient.

The cards are placed in small piles

Monopoly is my game.

During the morning

I'm told several times,

Not to Shout.

People complain and don't understand

Why I always have to win.

Autism and other problems,

Don't help.

Maybe next time we will not go to the

Library for practice.

By Christine Law

HOME THOUGHTS

She stands looking at the mirror

The walk to the bathroom is slow.

At seventy two years of age

She needs support.

John gave up on her years ago

He has met someone else.

She feels like the girl of twenty

He married.

Someone is knocking on the door

Screaming she opens the door.

Helena can see that it's meal time,

with fried fish, boiled potatoes and peas.

Sitting down to eat, Helena sighs

The staff at Trimble lodge,

Are kind and understanding

It's not like being independent.

By Christine Law

UNTITLED

I go to sleep with a teddy bear and wake up to a grizzly clawing at my chest and lie in agony until sunrise when I can finally take a breath where the crushing pain accumulated from fear and the paranoia dissipates.

And people ask me why are you tired?

I live with a monkey that straddles my shoulders constantly weighing me down to where I don't feel like cleaning, where I don't feel like walking, or even getting out of the bed, and I have to force myself to do so because I have obligations that must be met each day and dinner to cook for people who have no ability to take care of themselves even when I can hardly take care of myself.

And people ask me why is my hair a mess?

I never walk to the water's edge because there is a crippling fear of drowning in the depths of my own cradled lake that flows ceaselessly through my mind with currents that could drag a tornado ripping through the area to the murky and dark bottoms of the bed that I cry and flail ceaselessly in gasping for a breath of fresh air as I sink in anxiety.

And people ask me what's wrong?

I carry around tied to my arm a black balloon for every failure, every death, every tragic moment in my life that doesn't float with helium but drags me to the ground like a ball and chain as I am tied to my past of regret and hopelessness and can't find the right pair of scissors to free myself from the strings that grip tighter and tighter as I try to pull myself free from the mark of death that fades into my skin from previous attempts of cutting to loosen the bondages that hold me down.

And people ask why I am sad?

I free fall endlessly in a black hole that has no bottom, no relief of escape by death, no relief of help coming to save me from the torment of knowing that I am falling silently even though my mouth is open trying to scream the nightmare of my life away as the pit grows deeper and deeper, and I struggle for just a calming inhale, but the rushing wind steals each gasp from my lips as I open and close my mouth or try to steal a breath through my nose.

And people wonder why i do not speak often...

People ask me these things, and I tell them, and they never understand because they do not awaken with a grizzly, they do not fear the water, they do not have a monkey on their shoulders, they are not free falling into an endless black hole, and they can breathe freely without the anxiety and depression and suicidal tendencies floating through their heads as they struggle day to day just to exist, and they refuse to acknowledge these things and just smile and tell me things will be ok even when I stand before them falling apart, and they cannot see the strands of myself slip to the ground in silent notes of exhaustion...

By Kasey Hill

WHAT WOULD IT FEEL LIKE TO BRING THOSE WALLS DOWN?

What would it be like to bring those walls down?

Vulnerable, scary, terrifying

And who would even stick around?

Nobody would love me if they saw the real me

Don't love me with or without

But they'd hurt me by rejecting my honesty

I do have to learn to rely on others

And say what I want, feel and need

But the thought of opening up

Makes me feel like I can't breathe

My thoughts don't matter

They'd see how ugly, messed up and damaged I really am

But if I'm a protected person

I have nothing but don't give a damn

When you say what would that be like?

I can't sit with those thoughts and reflect

My stomach drops and I'm frightened

I'm scared of the numbness, I reject

By Louise

BOTTOM OF THE FOOD CHAIN

The pain cuts so deep

And yet I feel numb

There must be something about her

That made them choose her as their special one

She is their daughter

And I'm just in pain

I could never be comforted by cuddles

Or have my hair swept from my face

I wanted her to be loved and never to feel like me

Wanted her to have everything and know she could be anything she wanted to be

I was the rejected one who doesn't have a place

But she was worth it and that was written all over my face

They chose her, I would too

But why did nobody care about the pain I was going through

I could never compete but how could I even want to

Feeling jealous of her having a bigger chunk of nothing feels so selfish

I told her she looked beautiful because I wanted to feel beautiful

I wanted her to know she was smart

She could have a level of confidence, bravado, perhaps,

and self esteem

All I had was my bedroom, the chaos and my dreams

Dreams of getting out of there

Making something of myself

Stopping them from hurting my soul

And coming out of my shell

A Darker Shade of Blue

I was faking it too

The smile on my face

Was always happy, always joking

School was a safer place

But what did they unequivocally see in me

But without any thought

Emptiness was just there

and that was obvious

I was the disappointment and was angry as hell

Bad and dirty, a weird little shell

But that can't be what they saw in a baby

that's what *they* did

No belief in fairytales, life is what it is

Wanting to warn people off me

I'm damaged goods, I freak out

Not accepting love

And rejecting what real intimacy is about

Passively standing in the shower dissociating

And you didn't want to get in

Feeling scared of sex

Jumping when the doorbell rings

For me, being obsessed and disgusted by my smell

Feeling guilty for breathing

Painful mouth associations

..No one ever tells

Throat swells up, no water splashing on my face

Melt into music

That would be my escape

Then defensive anger, seeing rejection at every turn

Not Trusting my own judgement

The emptiness in my soul burns

It makes me more fragile

And it makes me strong

Learning to hear my memories, my feelings

And know that they, my protectors, were wrong

Feel outside of society

Like I m faking it but people can see

I m outwardly confident but that's not the real me

Excruciatingly empty

Feeling people stop and stare

I sit on the floor I'm more comfortable there

Lying around for days on end

Snap out of it

You are a survivor

I need to be my friend

By Louise

AN ODE TO ANXIETY

You make me nervous,

giving me Irritable bowel syndrome,

you give me stomach pains,

so I have to stay at home.

You make me have a fear

of going down the stairs,

I get stuck on the landing,

but I refuse to stay there.

You make my heart beat, my hands clammy

when I want to publicly speak,

so when I do say a word

it comes out as just a squeak.

Despite the IBS

the often trips to the loo,

the fear of heights,

I won't give in to you.

By Julie Day

BLACK DOG

That day:

The worst day of your life,

When it's all over

And you run, screaming,

Into a corner.

Dogged by life.

Afraid of the shadows

That chase you there.

And then,

From the shadows

Steps a dog.

Your dog?

Black eyes watching.

Your eyes.

Offering something that's

Not quite company.

He gives you excuses:

To walk and not walk,

To eat and not eat,

To sleep, sleep, sleep

In mimicry of him.

Until he growls,

A growl that shakes your soul.

Reminds you of how far

You'd have to go

To forget

That day.

When everything ended,

And the dog began.

So you chain him

In the yard.

But he barks at night,

Tearing hair from your scalp

With every bitter note.

And you give him

To the pound,

But he's still your dog.

Black eyes watching,

Panting in your ear.

The echo of ownership

Is still enough

To pull you in.

So you claim him back.

He comes when he is called,

But you are not his master.

Black eyes. Your eyes.

And the growl that's always waiting.

You drown him

In cold water.

Though he hurts you

And, in part,

You're drowning too.

And death puts no stopper

In his bark

Or in his bite.

The black dog

Came from

Your shadows.

And he will leave,

Only,

When you have

Seen the light.

By K.C. Finn

THE MASK I WEAR

I stand still outside your room

and force my face to smile —

Take deep breaths to steel myself

and I march inside.

You and I laugh together —

inconsequential mirth.

I gush words onto your lap

and push down my pain .

A single moment each day

and then I turn to go,

As I leave you never see

my mask slipping off.

By Claire Thomson

UNTITLED

Full of hopelessness and despair, I feel some people do not care.

I wake each day and wish the anxiousness and depression would just fade away.

It is hard to cope and such a struggle. Why is my head in such a muddle?

Waiting for some CBT. I feel it will be good for me.

It is causing me so much strife. All I want is a happy, simple life.

So many people want lots of wealth. All I want in life is good mental health.

By Christina Leach

ANXIETY

Standing on the platform trying to breathe,

Air stifling you like a front room in a heatwave.

Your heart pumping, blood bolting through your bones.

"It can't be good for me

To feel so revved up, to fear losing control,

Falling down. Even though I haven't ever."

Your legs want to buckle, like when

You're walking over a bridge high above the motorway.

"What if I can't stop them running to the edge

And I lurch over? Is that even likely to happen?

Is that what makes people jump in front of trains?"

The train is approaching.

You slow, slow your breath, your mind, your being.

"I don't feel that bad. But what if it gets worse?

What if I cry, scream, can't breathe, can't help it…".

Breathe. Out.

The train is slowing.

You stand up straight,

Make your feet step onto that train,

Walk as if... remember how it used to be?

The springing seat lulling you through the landscape

In daydreams of cities and seasides.

You can do it.

By Astrid Black

IN MY MIND

Some days seem dark

Some days seem light

In my mind

Without reference to the world outside

Sometimes the darkness drags on

Dragging for days, weeks

Dragging me down so deep

It seems light no longer exists

No escape is possible

But perhaps the worst days

Are the kaleidoscope days

Switching from light to dark

Light to dark, light to dark

Over and over

Taking what moments before

Seemed good

And rendering it vile and bleak

By D J Tyrer

D.I.D. AND ME

(Dissociative Identity Disorder, a complex form of P.T.S.D)

Hello,

can anybody hear me,

can anybody see me,

for who I really am?

My mother played the abusing part

she drove the life force from my heart,

my identity was ground to dust

and there was no one I could trust.

Hello,

Can anybody hear me,

can anybody see me,

for who I really am?

So I found new "parts" within me,

as the child inside had died,

they fought hard to protect me

and soon became my guide.

Hello,can anybody hear me,

can anybody see me,

for who I really am?

Parts got triggered, lies were said

the voices crossed inside my head.

I was targeted and criminalised

I was punished for "their" lies,

and so I became despised.

Please

will you all now hear me

will you see me

for who I really am?

I am a survivor of D.I.D

now I know what it is to be me.

I found an angel, a helper forever

who put all my "parts" back together.

The police did not hear me,

the courts did not "see" me

my friends abandoned me

for who they "thought I was".

Please now,

can you see us all

can you hear us all?

Accept now what is true –

We are all just like you.

By Anon

Note from author: This poem is dedicated to every person suffering from mental health issues, especially those who have been criminalised for it, and found no justice, - because there is no justice.

The justice system refuses to accept mental illness and we were disallowed DID in mitigation and therefore never got to tell our side of the story, yet statistics show that 48% of people on probation suffer from some form of identity disorder.

LITTLE ALBERT

Screams echoing in the

abandoned hospital,

Backwards To the sun

streaming

In at arched windows

On the monkey who

thought

He was Born to lead,

A march into utopia.

Progress always demands

blood,

Science claims as its

sacrifice

The innocence of

yesterday,

A parade of expandable,

Dolls in wire cages

Turning into crowds,

roaring

In a torch lit stadium.

You couldn't have guessed,

The dark century you

brought

To its bloody birth;

Its bombs and

barracks,

A homage to apes,

Too clever to be good.

By Adam Colclough

HERO

history will not name you a hero

a boy who fought dragons

grew to a man

put away a plastic sword

and took up a knife.

the dragons grew within you

unchecked by medication

curled around your bones

hid behind the grey scaled shadows

of your eyes

breathed fierce fire in blood betraying

self made wounds.

hero is a name without a face

courage painted by numbers

stories honoured in history's roll call

but your battle has no timed beginning

no ordered end

no truce

no ceasefire

no catalogue of reasons

no pages map the trench line scars

on your arms.

and when it ends

if it ends

there will be no flags

no cheers

no banners raised

if the dragons sleep

those who love you will not wake them

and if it is you who sleeps

I will remember you

in secret silence

By Karen Ankers

GREY TILL GREYER

This rectangle of sky, grey until greyer

Sits itching

Burning

Emptied out

Eyes follow the clumps of dirt, green growths

Outside my window

The plants gather nutrients, they are thirsty

They will thrive until they perish

Like all that blooms

Opening like a chimney's mouth

To soot of fire,

Decay

The eager colours washed away

In another flood

On another average, terribly average day

And generations of quick things

Until they are still

squirrels

Scampering along the fence

Bearing seeds and morsels of food

Sink their skinny bones

In clay

Mourning doves nesting in the eaves

Pretty to hawks

I saw a whole family taken

A few scattered feathers remained

A Darker Shade of Blue

My prayers have no grip

I wish I could forget

Everything, this sky

The futile things I will or won't

Time passing as it may

Grey until greyer

A palette of dismay

By Alex S. Johnson

SAILING WITH JOSEPH CONRAD

On this freezing road at speed

Mist patches pass briefly

While slight, sharp pains intimidate the heart.

Angina... Now you have a name,

Sounding like a saint or a virgin queen

Covered by black armour.

In middle age are my arteries are failing me?

The freezing stain of a frost sunset

Fades on the December skyline.

In the indistinct warmth of the car

I roll my head and look at a deeper shadow.

'I was born in that valley.' I say.

For years, decades, I have had no use

A Darker Shade of Blue

For the word depression, except to describe the weather.

Recently, I sleep badly and wake up wondering

Whether anyone can really be trusted,

And bad dreams lie heavily on my digestion.

Certainly, the bad weather crowds in,

Corrupting the smiles of my family;

Well-off, well-connected friends tell me to drink less.

Sadly, like most of the human race, I lack resources,

And so I postpone dealing with my sickness

To take to the streets to work one last time.

There is only the unlimited sky, the vastness

Conveyed to me by Joseph Conrad,

By Korzeniowski, a Polish seaman

Who became famous, an English classic;

The world read his books and did not care to guess

At his passionate despair.

There is only that nothingness,

The thing *he saw*, the thing *I saw*, at twelve years old,

The blank, receiving greyness to which this road will lead me...

Unless like him, sailing with no horizon visible,

A kind of stubbornness keeps me steering, steering

In the hope that one lighthouse can still be found.

By Anthony James

A WAY OUT OF THIS PAIN

I thought about

ending it once

or maybe more than

twice,

but eventually I found

my strength and my voice;

when my uncle

took his own life

I realised that I didn't want

to die

I just wanted a way out of this pain—

books, music, nature

are the things that heal me

more than the company of humans

because whilst some of them may

A Darker Shade of Blue

mean me well

I have met many who do not,

and so I have found

my healing is in the silence

of finding the words in my heart

putting them on paper

so all the world can see

they won't crush me because my nightmares

are darker than any of the things

they could give me.

By Linda M. Crate

WHEN ANXIETY ATTACKS

My anxiety

was out of control

could feel my heart as if it

were going to beat

out of my chest,

felt dizzy,

had to sit down;

my mind was screaming

with the ferocity

of a hurricane—

I remember

his mother just wouldn't be quiet

as if making me fret

was the flames that made her joy

burn at it's highest scream,

and I wanted nothing more than to

sew myself into silence;

nothing was quiet enough to ease

my suffering

until they forgot me on the stairs then

peace found me and my heart

eased to a calm—

later she tried to claim it was

a heart attack,

but I know it wasn't.

By Linda M. Crate

PERMANENCE OF DEATH

I wonder

where you'd be now

if you could've

just held on,

and I miss you,

uncle;

wish you could've found peace

that wasn't in the permanence

of death—

I wish you could've known

you were talented

maybe if you could've held out

you would've sold

more of your art

I think the internet could've helped

you there,

but you snuffed your candle out

before it could

shine;

now we'll never know—

I still have the last letter you wrote me

still have the last gift you gave,

and every time I see grey skies

I think of the grey of your eyes;

wishing they could fix me in the softness of their

gaze once more.

By Linda M. Crate

I DON'T ALWAYS FEEL STRONG

The birds are singing

flowers are forgiving,

and I find slants

of sunshine yet I cannot

force myself

out of bed

despite how much I tell myself

there's a lot that needs to

be accomplished;

an hour or two later I crawl

out of bed

angry at the time I wasted

unable to focus

finding myself to be

nothing less

than a failure

have to remind myself to breathe—

some days are harder

than others

some days I feel brave

for simply facing the day

because I don't always feel as strong

as I am

sometimes I don't know the light

that comes with dawn

until someone reminds me

of the light in my heart.

By Linda M. Crate

WHEN I WAS A GIRL

Pacing the room

anxious as can be

I remember

being scolded by

my father

Sitting on the couch

unable to stop

myself from the tendency

to fidget

I remember being scolded

by my father

As if this is something

I had any

control of,

but when I said I couldn't help it

he always insisted

I could;

As if I were simply lying

for the sake of

doing so—

maybe he didn't understand

the labyrinth of my mind

all my anxiety, all of my despair;

but he didn't have to be so cruel

He broke me with the

thorns of his anger and his nightmares

because once he was broken

instead of breaking the cycle

he broke me

which is the reason my depression consumed

me so thoroughly when I was a girl.

By Linda M. Crate

BLACK DOG

Uninvited, unwanted he nevertheless arrives

To wreak havoc with my day

My antennae predict his coming

But do not reveal how long he will stay

I clean the house, buy fresh flowers

Light candles. Prepare for my unwelcome guest

Cancel parties. Take the phone off the hook.

Paint my nails. Dress in my best.

Resist his visit, he is fiercely tenacious

Shows me yellow teeth, issues a warning growl

Now compliant, his reluctant hostess

Must indulge his predacious prowl

A Darker Shade of Blue

Come, I exhort him, sit here by my hearth

Warm your dangerous flanks by my fire

My house is your house for the duration

Take whatever you desire

Toss my mind about like an old slipper

 Gnaw at my bones. Feast on my heart.

Let my tears quench your thirst. Devour my soul.

 Only then will you stealthily depart.

By Jeannie Sloman

TEMPEST

It's unexpected.

That piercing pain.

A stabbing ache.

The warning of something yet to come.

A dark omen

as a black cloud on my horizon

then it's gone.

The sun appears;

the day brightens.

I carry on regardless;

move through the morning

like nothing ever happened

and I smile.

Then it's back again.

The storm descends full force.

Obsidian clouds with lightning strikes.

I gasp for air;

hitched breaths

as an inferno in my chest.

I regress.

I rasp and wheeze.

I silently plead,

I beg,

Count 1, 2, 3....

I ride the tempest of my deepest fears

Until that black mist disappears.

By T. F. Webb

SMACK

The needle punctured my fleshy bruised skin,

Another missed vein a source of my agony.

Tried yet again and connected for the win,

My perception of now a slow dying reality.

The warmth of a cocktail coursing my veins

My eyes rolling up causing a brain haze.

This of my soul is all that remains,

As heavy and bloodshot my eyes a fixed gaze.

Closer to death's door my guardian awaits

Determining my worthiness at God's Pearly gates

The Grim Reaper too is close by my side

Determining if he will be my guide.

A pounding chest is my reality check

Surrounded by white and halos in sight

My name being called. Mr Beck?Mr.Beck?

"Come on, Come On, You can fight, Fight Fight."

Chest is pounding and my vision becomes clear

Paramedics overtop of me and lanterns shed lite

Gambling with smack is now something to fear

My final destination I know I must make right

As angels above

Demons below

Send me a dove

This that I know.

By Matthew Mikituk

THE HOST

As Urial descended upon his corrupted soul

The meek and impoverished being unbeknownst to thee

Accepting the empowered Angels integration for sight

The being now fully consumed by light

Unknowingly now, the guided being to be

Carefully selected to remove the demon infested soul

From his will and his mind, another God be

Introduced to his soul God willingly

In the name of Basu, I formally cast you

From this beings free will and true destiny.

Demons and Angels fight a holy war.

The henchmen still here from a long time ago,

Since the appearance of man through every nation

Many unknowingly susceptible to integration.

As parasites infect unwilling hosts

Summoning henchmen of long lost ghosts

All cultures and all beliefs aside

The choice can be yours, if you abide.

By Matthew Mikituk

WHEN THE LIGHT HAS GONE

Where does he go? I cannot follow

Into the darkest recesses of his mind

I long to shine a light into his world

A world that I no longer inhabit.

He has a label pinned to him now

Dementia is the word they use

It means nothing to him

It means a world of loss to me.

There are fleeting glimpses of the old John

They are becoming rare

So many dark days now

When the light seems to have gone out completely

I miss his touch, his laugh, his wit

But my pain is as nothing to his

When in those few lucid moments

He maybe realises his torment

I am as helpless as he

To stem the tide

Which sweeps him inexorably into oblivion.

By Dorothy Snelson

A SECOND CHANCE

The deepest and darkest feelings interrupted my life.

Despair, sadness, hurt.

A new beginning full of positivity, a new life.

Relief, joy, optimism.

By Rebecca Leemon

DEPRESSION

You do not barge in suddenly

like an irritating guest born to give headaches

You are not violent like a raging storm,

ripping tiles from my roof,

felling my trees of reality.

Rather like a whirlwind,
you dance as you move ever closer.
Your ghost hovers on the horizon
Until you move in.

Wiping your ugly boots on my days and nights.

Trampling over my threadbare mind

until I can only sit and stare and wait for you to leave.

Wondering how much you will take with you

Fearing how little

of my exhausted friends,

my confidence

my reason

will be left to carry on

No, you do not barge in suddenly.

You settle insidiously like poisonous snow

Freezing the marrow of my existence,

Leaving me like dirty sludge on the the side of the road.

Sanity disfigured and

disgraced.

My battered body tries to knit together,

and clatter on,

clumsily at first,

then silently.
Pausing only to peer for signs of dust on the horizon.

Knowing you will be back.

Not knowing when.

By Lynne Chitty

THE SALESMAN

He rings her bell. He knows just when to call

For him, she pretends that she's not in

Rap! Rap! He won't give up, he won't do that

It's his calling card, his familiar grin

'Hello, again, it's me, it's Mr A.'

'And I'm Miss B,' she says. 'So go away

I do not care for what you have to say.'

But already he's half inside her door

As before, she expects what's coming next

And he enters in his usual, brutal way

Through her cortex. Look what he's brought today:

Some depression, a few disordered thoughts

And one nightmare panic attack. How's that?

'Yes, but I don't buy your wares,' says Miss B

'It's too late; they're planted now,' says Mr A

'Let's watch them grow.' And, as she does, they do.

'So here's my inclusive, all-intrusive

Head-steal-deal. Just for you I'll throw in too

Some pills, some booze, some compulsive rituals

All at my knock-out rate.' He reels the take:

She swallows the fly from his toxic hook

And she lines his palm with all the calm

All the still, unbroken bits that are left

Behind in her duped and suckered mind

That is the way with Mr Theory A1

She prays that on the day when he returns

She will learn to win and she won't be in

She'll be in a place that's safe and free

---

[1] In Cognitive Behavioural Therapy, Theory A is the term which describes the faulty basis for believing the negative thoughts associated with mental health conditions such as depression and anxiety disorders.

And that is Theory B2. The therapy.

By Morna Clements

---

2 Theory B is the therapeutic contrasting viewpoint, which promotes a positive/realistic outlook and challenges the destructive power of Theory A.

GREEN LANE

fear b u b b l e s in my

stomach

this body's all out of

sync with life

i've never been so

alone

as this

my fate

entrusted to strangers

i sit

desolate

upon the bed

inside the room with

anaemic walls

that are closing in with every

b r e a t h

i cannot cry

i do not feel

my life is not a play which

holds a role for me

i am stripped of all that once I was

because I am rotten

they tell me i'm ill

not safe to be

alone

and so they watch me

like i am entertainment

i watch me too

as i do all that i am told

with no questions no

w

  o

   r

   d

  s

i am destroyed by the

shocks

that burn

compliance

into my brain

they leave me vacant

hazy

heavy

lost

d e a d

i wonder if i will ever escape

i wonder if i really care

By Rachel Peck

THE A-Z OF DEMENTIA

Anger was the trigger. Of course it was.

Beating yourself up. We all do it.

Carer. What exactly does that mean?

Dynamics. Family dynamics in constant flux.

Ego. People don't like this word.

Fury. Carer's Fury. F is also for Forgive. So I am working on that one.

Going out. This was the biggie.

Help. None of us wants to be a nuisance, do we.

Independence. What a beautiful word that is.

Jollying along. We've all done that, haven't we.

Kidding ourselves. Next year it will all be better.

Living the life. It's not, is it?

Mother. She told me, "You've got to be the mummy now."

No. The word we have to practise.

Other people. This can incorporate anybody other than yourself.

Personal hygiene. "I like my baths."

Questions. Every day is a question.

Responsibility. A grown up word.

Seeing things that are not there. My dad came and sat next to her one afternoon. He has been dead over twenty years.

Time. "What day is it?"

Upset. "You haven't been in to see me for quite a few days."

Very forgetful. The next time we will go through the process again.

Where do we go from here? Who knows?

X-rays. I did get confused as to why one part of the hospital couldn't get through on the phone to another part. But we all get there in the end.

You. Or is it me?

Z is for Zen

By Sarah Crabtree

Note from author: *Good luck and happiness to us all!*

MY BEAUTIFUL BABY GIRL

I lay awake at night –

Listening

Listening for sounds, both real and imaginary

Listening to my body wrestling under the blanket in frustration,

Listening to my nostrils as they take deep, deliberate inhalations and exhalations.

I lay awake at night

Waiting,

Wanting for you to cry out for me.

My excuse to get up,

My cover-up for another sleepless night.

But you never do.

You never call out for me.

You're my dream sleeper,

And I'm the Idiot who can't sleep.

What's wrong with me?

I wasn't like this with your brother.

I don't feel like myself.

And yet I have no tears,

So I must be okay.

I'm so ashamed,

I can't tell anyone.

Your daddy says it's all in my head.

I try to empty out my head

But I fail.

I'm no good at anything anymore.

I'm just a jittery collection of random, pointless thoughts and images.

Flipping unlimited channels on a TV

But the off button's broken.

The flipping won't stop.

Sometimes,

After I have been up all night,

I watch out the window as the light first invades the darkness,

As the morning sounds break the silent stillness of the night.

I watch you, my beautiful baby girl

I watch you sleep.

I wait for you to wake.

I feel Guilty,

Guilty for not being fresh and alert for you.

When you smile at me,

Or hold out your arms for me,

I am surprised.

I don't know why you love me.

I haven't done anything to deserve your love.

But thank you for loving me back

My beautiful baby girl.

Thank you.

I will be better for you.

I will get better for you.

My beautiful baby girl.

By Nazneen F. Jafferi

THE SITUATION AND THE SOLUTION

There was a man there was a boy

the man treated the boy like he was a simpleton and a toy

the man made the shadows snarl and grin

the man killed dreams and soaked his hands in blood and sin

the man made dark voices and shot them into the boy's head

the man troubled the boy until the boy felt like he was almost dead

one day the boy rose up and decided to risk a true fall

the boy went to the man and his pain hungry kind and said "I will hug you all"

it was known that the delusions of the boy were vigorous and loud but the boy did something that would always make himself proud

when one day he was a new kind of man

a growing warrior with a master plan

he had a hug for each devil and each devil's tool

he had a hug for everyone downtrodden or lost and a hug for each fool

the boy turned new man went on to see his problems come to a gradual end

as the boy turned new man wanted to hug everyone and call them friend

By Butch Parrow

THE HOLLOW BEAST

The hollow beast comes fast with blows, bites and hits

Doesn't check your schedule—you'll make room for him

Repeatedly, he feasts on essence

Then why is he so thin?

Presumably, the constant motion

Keeps the pounds off

By Alex S. Johnson

MY MIND IS A MILLION PIECES

I'm just next to you

like an oxygen you breath,

steeped in the stream of hedonism,

you can't see my bitter tears.

World as a cauldron

on the fire of awareness,

it aspires to omniscience,

but doesn't want to understand.

Thoughts of a better future

and a light that distracts the darkness –

I'd like to take them off the shelf of infirmity,

in vain, the weight of depression overwhelms the hands.

My mind is a million pieces,

I try to put them together each day,

in a world of hypocritical clichés

it's easy to lose the smallest part.

by Norbert Gora

WHICH WAY

A hum-drum existence

and a daily grind;

it feels ok.

Then wham bam! Brain boils over

thoughts whizz and race

as the eye of a camera flickers.

Recording multi images

layered across a screen

of multitude colours

shone through a varifocal lens.

The speakers emit thunder claps as

hi-fi voices batter ears,

a cacophony of noise bombards the brain.

Working at double speed the mind

struggles to disentangle multi messages.

Racing through a hundred places,

A Darker Shade of Blue

no conclusion in sight,

nothing to staunch the flow but a

further urge to run and discover -

lost on an endless journey.

Exhausted at last, fall in a heap,

lost in a pool of pale blue tears.

Acknowledge the fears,

haul up a familiar track.

Bid farewell to past's heedless hell,

salute modest clarity and inch slowly forward.

By Jane Findley

IN THE MOMENT

The darkness can swallow you whole,

tear you to shreds.

And spit you out in a lonely place.

You want to die in the moment, but forever?

You want to shine again.

You pick up the pieces time after time.

Losing one, then another;

a part of you lost altogether.

You want to die in the moment, but forever?

You want to shine again.

The pain grows deeper, the words turn sour.

The venom poisons,

then devours.

A Darker Shade of Blue

You want to die in the moment, but forever?

You want to shine again.

Your stomach growls, you want it over.

Cajoled by the devil

sat on your shoulder.

You want to die in the moment, but forever?

You want to shine again.

You survive the night; a new day's dawning.

The rough seas have parted

but heed this warning:

You shine in the moment, but forever?

Darkness will fall again.

By Hannah Ellis

ANOTHER TWITCHING SLEEP

A breath,

so tragic in its incompleteness

heaved in and out.

Relief, to catch the apex of that lungful.

Relax, an unwise voice would say,

then, I would cease to function,

waste another day.

There was some great, dark secret there to be uncoiled

within the climax of that damned elusive breath.

I'll take my death

if dreams could be of gentler stuff,

of silver streams

and woods that murmur where my mother sings.

My dreams,

they were not dark.

A Darker Shade of Blue

In glorious colour they would tilt and laugh

blood covered loved ones

with the wounds I keep …

I gouged the nails of Christ …

but they had sunk too deep!

Why did I wake, when I was not asleep?

So, even now I fear the fall of night

that gentle time when rest should heal

the peacefulness that spiteful creature's steal.

Come restless ones,

together we shall wait the morning light.

I should have suffered even more

If I knew then that time would make it right.

By Lois Hambleton

DEPRESSION

He's sitting here on my sofa

Here but curiously not really all there

He tries to make conversation, be a good guest

But I can see the effort it takes and to be fair

He needs help, professional help, but he lacks the courage and motivation to seek it

And I. his friend, don't know how to break through,

Can't think how to help and my frustration grows even though, I know

It's not his fault. We literally have no idea what to do.

He's been sleeping in his car,

Swapped that for the sofa which at least is somewhere to be

That he can rest better, have a shower, eat something hot

Find company to lift his mood and be distracted a bit by the TV

If only for a while. He says this is helping

Smiles a little, chats about his kids and how they do at school

Talks, wiping tears, about his marriage his shattered dreams of family life

How he didn't see the problems or the end in sight, how he feels like a fool

He's lying here on my sofa and I try to sit still, to let him sleep

He's here but strangely absent too

I know he needs to move on, that this is no long-term solution

But I'm uncertain, worried, if only I could see more clearly what I need to do

By Felicity Middleton

TODAY, I HAVE A WORRY

Today I have a worry

It consumes my mind

and destroys my motivation.

My worry is irrational,

yet it does not stop.

Nothing has changed in my life:

today is the same as yesterday

only this day, I have a worry.

Right now it feels as though

my entire life will be dedicated

to my worry.

Yet I have had worries before;

different worries

that all felt the same as this worry.

They passed,

and this one will, too.

It might be this afternoon,

it might be tomorrow,

it might be in a month from now.

Today, I have a worry.

But someday, I will be okay.

By Ellen Grace

RUNNING

Dressed and ready

New trainers on my feet

Music on, tracker started

Heading towards the door

My head says no

Says "come on, don't go"

I wander the hallway

Thinking of all the ways

I can just sit and watch TV

I hope nobody sees me

Takes 45 minutes to leave the house

First run of the week, no stopping me now.

By Gareth Johns

MONEY

Money makes me happy

I love it when I have it

I hate being skint

I can't break the habit

Speaking of which, I don't drink, I don't smoke

I just sit in my mind, trying not to think

Bills keep rising, I try not to cry

Too many people I love, thought once "what if I die?"

So I struggle on, with no money at all

Sold my Camera, can't ask for help, sold it all

My heads a mess, I laugh and I joke

I can't see the end of the tunnel.

Can only see it going up in smoke.

By Gareth Johns

TAPS

My unmanned Dad who ran from the midlands,

turned greased elbows to handy jobs and plumbing-

he yearned to fix my balance and unbecoming eyes.

 All thumbs, he fitted green copper taps each side

and bulked my pipes out with lavender and teddy eyes,

but when one hinky tap dripped to a halt

the other leaked an assault, leading to symptoms

Dad couldn't apprehend. The cold feed would feel it's way

into head and hands while I cornered the bathroom

mirror, with my heavy head resting on my left shoulder.

I filled till I flooded with titanic shanks of ice,

bluing my lips and turning my words to garbling

fits. In secret, in blackness. I would drain my system,

bleeding pipes and flushing valves, pulling copper flakes from

my scalp hoping to release pressure. Once free of

ice, a moment of quiet always overtook. Then always;

the hot tap took its turn, kissing steamed air into ears

and lips, demanding to be held before an audience while it made me

dance into walls.

By Charlotte Begg

UNTITLED

She gave him all her love, but in return he broke her heart

A heart she gave to him which he tore apart

She gave him her trust, thought he'd love her till she died

But he twisted every word she said, as if each one were a lie

She turned deaf ears to others gave him the benefit of the doubt

Oh how she wishes she listened, listened and heard them out.

She gave him her life and he killed her day by day.

She wants to lose her memory and wipe him clean away

She wants to go so far away and say "I no longer have to see

All the times he dominated and belittled me!"

Sometimes she wants to cry, but her tears no longer fall

Catch her in thoughtful moments and her face will say it all.

She wants to sleep, but he is haunting all her dreams

She now knows that with him nothing was what it seemed

But now there is another, offering her his heart

The chance to leave the past behind, a change of a new start

But can she learn to trust him as she\s spinning all her plates

Can she let him close enough for friendship, or to be best mates

Maybe he could take away all the hurt, now that would be bliss

maybe in a magic moment, he'd seal love with a kiss

His writing reaches deep inside her , poetry that takes hold of her soul

He understands things about her, things he shouldn't know

He shares songs with thoughtfulness, words that touch her heart

Tears fall one by one, then a torrent once they start

And if he was there before her, and whispered out her name

Would life be so much happier never to be bad again?

He writes that he could protect her and for her always care

Oh can she dare imagine his fingers running through her hair?

He tells her that he loves her, loves her very much

Can she dare to dream about the magic of his touch?

Dare she reach out and take his hand that he offers now to her,

Does she understand that to her he will defer?

Can life and love be better than what she had before,

Has she got the courage to dare to hope for more,

Will she take a chance on him, have a future, start again

For this is now the present, her other life was then

By Bill

DEAR FRIENDS WITH ANXIETY...

That feeling over you of impending doom,

The feeling of dread, the feeling of gloom.

It follows you round like a little black cloud,

You suffer the fears of getting stuck in a crowd.

Always a constant battle inside the mind,

Something you really struggle to leave behind.

Every morning you stand, and you put on your mask.

And you hide that you struggle with day to day tasks.

Upon your face you've planted a big fake smile,

And it's an extremely good one, you've practised a while.

You can feel so isolated and incredibly alone,

And you hurt can't shake it, like a dog with a bone.

But keep on fighting, and don't ever stop!

As that is the only way you can go from rock bottom to top.

Think of how successfully, these battles you hide.

And how many people are on the same ride?

Anxiety/Depression your cover is blown!

I promise you friend, you are not on your own!

By Natalie Robinson-Bramley

DESTINY CAN NOT BE CHANGED

Everything in life is for a reason,

whether its love betrayal or treason.

All part of lessons we must learn,

Sometimes it hurts sometimes they burn.

In the end it'll make you strong,

Even when it all feels wrong.

Sometimes there's things we just don't know,

Whether to hold on or just let go.

But in the end it'll all become clear,

And the sign of an answer will appear.

Then we realise why these choices are made,

And that there's never a reason to be afraid.

Just let life continue its course,

And when you fall off, get back on the horse.

Because all of our paths are decided by fate,

Even when it doesn't seem all that great!

By Natalie Robinson-Bramley

THE INSIDE OF AN ANXIOUS MIND

Sometimes you can get a little lost

Sometimes you pay the ultimate cost

Nothing's worth more than those who care

The ones who love and with you they share

Your blinded by the dark

Your swimming from the shark

The darkness follows you all of the way

Until it's all night and there is no day

But you see a glimmer, a tiny light

Chase it and don't stop til it shines bright

Because when your dragged into that hole

It's your self preservation it stole

Only you can pull yourself back up again

It's your mind, your body, your brain

So believe that it will end no matter how gripping

Lift up your head princess, your crown is slipping

By Natalie Robinson-Bramley

ALLOW YOURSELF TO LOVE

There can be no wisdom without any pain,

Like there's no anger without any blame.

There can be no hurting without any dark,

Hard to have arguments without any bark.

There can be no happy without a smile,

Or laughing and giggling for a while.

There can be no soulmates without the love,

To feel you'd move the world and heaven above.

So open your eyes and let love flow through your blood,

Because nothing in life will ever feel this good

By Natalie Robinson-Bramely

GOOD ALWAYS OUTWEIGHS EVIL

The world today is full of terror and fear,

Whether it's far away or somewhere near,

What kind of world do our children see,

That all depends on you and on me.

It's no good to judge and no good to hate,

To our young children this doesn't look great,

Look for the good and the people who care,

The ones who have nothing but still want to share,

Teach them to focus on these people only,

Then they will know they'll never be lonely.

We look after each other, and stand together,

There will be good in this world, now and forever

By Natalie Robinson-Bramley

PIANO

The lonely piano plays in the distance

It's sound mournful and sad

The fevered mind hears it's call

And wandering it strains towards it

Through the desert the man wanders

And it always stays beyond reach

Locked away in the soul of the afflicted

The man stumbles, bleeding, torn

All is gone, all is gone

And the man shouts to the heavens

All is gone

A single tear falls from his eye

No one can understand why

The lonely piano plays in the distance

Its sound mournful and sad

By Mark Smith

LOVE IS PAIN

You stole from me like Codasil Coates

A bitter pill to swallow

It stuck in my throat

Me, highway robbery

You, heart theft yobbery

I love you,

You said

Messed with my head

Me, led up the garden path

You, oblivious of the aftermath

Carrying on after a love crash

Little value

Petty cash

Me, heart broken

You, devoid of emotion

I can't bear it

It hurts!

Emotional subverts

Me, I'm a wreck

You, took a rain check

Love unrequited

Flame unignited

No longer united

Me, wailing like a banshee

You, plenty more fish in the sea

By Nichola O'Hare

Pi

My heart it beats at 22 over 7

A tiny bit of mathematical heaven

An irrational number

Can't be expressed as a fraction

An anomaly dressed as a distraction

A statistical randomness

3.14 ampleness

A transcendental number

Pi equals c over d

The only thing on which we agree.

By Nichola O'Hare

YOUR ACERBIC WIT

Your acerbic with makes others feel shit

Often profound but not funny

But right on the money

It cuts like a knife and causes strife

But you're oblivious to this

When you're taking the piss

You're words, they hurt

Waspish and curt

But well thought out

To give maximum clout

You're like a venomous snake

A small scale earthquake

The words that you utter

Make your victims squirm and stutter

I don't condone the way that you talk

The way you cut down your prey like a drug addled hawk

But I admire your disambiguation

The way a train stops at a station

A social function

Pausing only at junctions

Facilitating brain traction

for your own satisfaction

A human time bomb

Wit delivered with aplomb

I admire you and your sense of no regret

Your brain is your biggest asset

People often say 'I wish I'd said that'

L'esprit de l'scalier at the drop of a hat

If only we all had your mind

In comparison our intellect is resigned

To the mundanity of life - unstreamlined

Regardless of this

You have a soft side

A part of you I love, that you hide

You are kind and funny

You don't care about money

You're clever, uncomplicated

You should be celebrated

I adore you my sweet

You make me complete

By Budgie Burgess

MY FAVOURITE PLACE (BLACK MOUNTAINSIDE)

Ok this is my favourite place

Where no one can reach me

My fingers move

Cold and

Hammer like

The notes mix and bounce

On clean walls

Loose and ragged they have a certain pace

Which gives life

To this moment

This place

How do I get there

Must I sell my soul

Maybe just a little each and every year

Until

There I am

At this place

An abstract picture

Hangs above my head

Purple

The grey light filters in

Through a smogged city window

Into a bare

Pale blue and pine room

My foot rests

On bare floorboards

To steady

The unarmed chair in which i sit

A nervous smile

Is quickly replaced

As a single tear

Runs down my face

I'm getting there

It's all falling into place

She enters the room

And watches in disbelief

Our eyes meet

Crystal blue on green

Time stands still

I drop my head in concentration

Years of practice pay off

As the music continues

Effortlessly

Crisp

Clear , loud and strong

It fills the room

Surrounding us

Bringing us together

Again I look

Into her eyes

And then beyond

The music resonates

And lifts us upwards

Spiralling

Slowly

Until we can look down

On this scene

This place

Outside

Far below

The city grinds on

Unaware of this moment

This Place

We are enclosed

In the arms of a loving child

Tears of joy and pure passion flow

A moment like this

This place

Most will never savour

Nor dare understand

I am not alone

This is my favourite place.

By D J Taylor

I THOUGHT ABOUT YOU

I thought about you today and the day before

I'll think about you tomorrow

And forever more

I thought about you last night

Before I went to sleep

I cried into my pillow

A gentle, silent weep

I thought about you this morning

When I saw the sunlight shine

Sun that will never feel the same in your life or in mine

 I thought about you at lunchtime

And how you've touched my heart

The hurt and pain you're feeling

Now that you're apart

I thought about you this evening

A Darker Shade of Blue

Sat quietly on my own

Just needing to tell you

You'll never be alone

I'll think about you at bedtime

And in the morning once again

I'll think about you for always

In my thoughts you will remain

By Elizabeth Betsie Armstrong

MY TEDDY

If my teddy could remember what would she think,

Would love me or hate me or get me a shrink.

If my teddy could talk what would she say,

Would she keep all the secrets I tell her each day.

If my teddy could move what would she do,

Would she hug me slap me or find someone new.

If my teddy was missing what would I do,

Be searching or crying or talking to you.

By Zara Hardy

SOME CALL ME

You call me Fat so I stop eating

You call me Ginger so I die my hair

You call me 4 eyes so I get contacts

You call me Stupid so I stop trying

You call me Spotty so I hide my face

You call me ugly so I wear makeup

You call me a Scruffy so I wear trendy clothes

You call me a slag so I cover up

You call me Fake so I try a new look

You call me a whore so I don't talk to boys

You call me a liar I can't take much more...

You wish I would Die,

I try, good bye.

By Zara Hardy

EXCALIBUR

I came across Excalibur whilst walking through the night,

The blade was sterling silver that shines and glistens bright.

The hilt was gold as pure as light with rubies as red as blood,

Oh what a sword that cleaved the hoards and survived through rain and flood.

King Arthur stood as I am now staring

At the sword the blade of silver in the stone with merlin

At the gourd oh what it would be to wield the sword that medieval legend tells,

Extract from clasp to reveal all power and cancel evil spells.

By A.M. Brogan

THE BIG, BLACK HORSE

Depression has no rhyme or reason.

It happens quicker than the changing of a season.

Self-loathing, doubt and insecurities!

These are depression's specialities.

Fine one minute and all it takes -

Is a wrong word or deed, and in its wake.

The spiral starts -

And in your heart of hearts.

You feel its darkness beginning to spread.

Filling you up from your toes to your head!

You try to stop it, you build a dam!

But depression crushes it with a slam!

Those around you don't understand or see.

Snap out of it, cheer up, they cry with glee!

If you could, you would.

You know that you should.

If only it was that damn simple.

Take a pin and pop that pimple!

You try, you fail, you make it worse.

Galloping that spiral on a big, black horse.

Darkness and suffering is its game.

Depression is its name!

By Nicola Antoniou

I AM NOT ME! (A SOLDIERS LIFE)

I joined and I am still me

I train and I am still me

I am deployed and I am still me

I protect and I am still me

I serve and I am still me

I fight and I lose me

I am battle scarred and I am no longer me

I am lost and I am not me

I am buried and I am finally free

By Nicola Antoniou

ANXIETY

Eyes are the windows to the soul.

Eyes everyday, everywhere,

Looking and judging.

Or are they?

Headphones in, walk brisk.

The eyes follow.

And yet some are happy.

They judge in a positive light.

Walk tall, breathe steady.

Let them know you are proud.

And let yourself know it.

You are stronger than their diagnosis.

For you are much more than they perceive you to be.

By Laura Robson.

For my friend K

FOR DEL.. A SCOTTISH MUSE

Once upon a time I slightly lost my vision.

Forever hiding I now know is not quite right

And has become some foolish mission.

In a funny old pit stop,

the one I like to call,

the masses are amusing,

Peering and observing every last straw

what they don't see is really quite simple.

The quieter and observant become visible once more.

This feeling in which I understand has become everybody's

muse.

How many fuses do they think I have to blow,

before they are completely amused?

Bright upon this timeless taste,

I shall never hunt for a cure.

I will rest within this wondrous place

To follow adventures that will inevitably lead to fate.

By Ceri Wilkins

TIRED, BORED

Bored, bored, tired, bored, bored, bored, tired, bored, pain, blind, tired, bored, ouch, head, tired, bored, here, now, tired, bored, thinking, being, tired, bored, wanting, feeling, tired, bored, badger, nonsense, tired, bored, loving, needing, tired, bored, always, hoping, tired, bored, living, stamina, tired, bored- Boring, Tiredness

Tired, Bored!

By Ceri Wilkins

EQUALING....

Who and what is worth knowing.
Life turns, spins in roundabouts,
Everyone has a different story.
There's shit, it improves, leading to the result.
But which one is worth knowing?
When the world isn't willing to care.
Looking at the one who is maybe waiting for....

All the other clocks are laughing at me,
Cause I'm different.
Neither here nor there
Sits the narcoleptic insomniac.
Wondering how to create and explore brain power
And randomly situating art amongst the many collages
attached to the brain.

The connection of thoughts to happiness creates files of
insignificance through significance.
What about The Tales Of Today amongst the state of literal
existence.
It flows and never ends.
And so you think...
But out the buts and throw away the maybes because it just
is!

You put them in some MENTAL BIN and consider how to
blag a blagger.
You look towards the significance of sadness, maybe
building some bridges and reviewing the memories.

Then you wonder...

Where have all the letters gone?
Who do you know?
Celebration? Whatever!

A sudden STOP!
At every house before I get to your door.
Being a sudden understanding @bored.com

They say, you say, I say, we're too extreme for each other.
How I think of u.
They seek new places and view old faces,
Spending some time with forever friends.
Now I remember why I don't watch television!

So I figure I've cleared my head so much it's crashing.
Crashing to rebuild.
Looking at the point.
Oh how I love you and don't blame you for everything thats
in hand.
I'm sorry you, my mum.

The nightmare into the dealable.
How strange security and freedom start linking.
The issues to face,
Your head's all over the place,
Driven crazy by pure hecticness.

I can feel pain, STUPID HEAD lives in a dream.
Life is everywhere once again.

Time to sort it,

Realism possibilities,
Divided by strokes.

Divided by or EQUALING?

Maybe if you talk about what's bothering you, you won't
have to sulk or suck up!

Rainbow Rice...create and to explore brain power, keep
learning, forever expanding, till maybe one day you just
stopped and found what it was you were looking to learn in
the first place.
If I am the Jack of diamonds then i am not placing myself
top rank but high enough.

Thoughts of today...
Stability to do what I want and need for myself.
Progression into the motivation to keep the need for
freedom and independence.
Today is weary, tiring and complete.
My brain appears to be a different shape, triangular? Oh
dear
My mind may work better alone,
Keeping in the understanding you just know,
Without belittlement.

I hope your enjoying this happiness you seem to be gaining
from my pure boredom!
Manners and smiles cost nothing...
Have the openness to learn, listen and understand,
Now is time for progress.

Until...

Your taking the piss,
Think about the times,
Think about the pleasure,
Think about the feelings,
The past, present and future.
How much stress to you all need to inflict beforew you
realise how much you can rip someone apart with one foul
mouth.
Never mind with physical behaviour.
It's petty stupid and insensitive.
Other people have a right to feel loved, wanted and
needed.
It's not always your selfish right.
It's not always about only you,
Think about somebody else for a change.

By Ceri Wilkins

KEEP TELLING YOURSELF YOU ARE OK

I was always too scared to be seen as bad and wrong,
If mistakes were made then consequences would scare.
Closure and hiding become apparent.
Abuse of personal being,
Now no longer with need to hide.
Inner thoughts push towards protection and rightfulness.
Inner self reminds you your ok because you are...

Who's business is who's?
I hear you say,
I didn't know and wasn't aware
We were supposed to share until later.
But now everyone knows,
So what?
Who care's?
How extreme to we have to go?
Before we are content.
Extremity versus humanity.
It's not a competition you know.
Smile-xxx
So as you can see siting here just here is very random and
hectic for me.
Always passing the buck,
Never realising the disappearance of true lies.

This is my rant
This is my book
This is my thoughts
This is my plans
This is my future

This is my exploration
This is me so far and yet to come
This is where my writing began

By Ceri Wilkins

(Note from author: grass will grow on my hands before she
makes any sense!)

HOW ARE YOU?

"How are you " I'm fine I say, will live to fight another day.

This front this act is what I do, to make it seem that I'm like you.

I'm not ok I feel so low, but that's what I don't want you to know.

I'm down I'm beat I'm fighting a war, but all of this behind closed doors.

I don't think straight I try so hard to beat this thing I have found,

Depression anxiety pain and more is what I struggle to live for.

My fight is real but ill hide it from you, to keep the judges away that follow you.

The stigma attached is often wrong, you're mental , a psycho or just plain wrong.

If only people saw life through my eyes, they would maybe see and be surprised,

That im stronger than I look, braver than most and fighting this thing isn't a joke.

My strength will come and I will win for I won't be beaten by this thing.

Il fight back and prove you wrong, you won't keep me down long.

So yes I may hide it but more so for me, so I can see where I should be.

In a happy place not low and down, fighting back and claiming my ground.

What's depression anyway?

It is normal I am not odd it just makes me a special kind weird.

I want my life back stronger than before and this time il give it what for.

So next time you say how are you?

Just think what they may go through

By Luke Thompson

IF THE MIND WAS A TENT

If the mind was a tent

Then PTSD, depression and anxiety

Are the storm

Friend and family become the pegs

That hold us to the ground

Sometimes the storm rages

Through the dark of night

A couple of pegs could become loose

But the storm will pass and

The better the pegs

The better the tent will be in the morning

Old or new

It's the pegs that stop the tent from tearing

Itself apart in the storm

I'm grateful for them all

Look after your friends

They are your pegs

By Matthew Wightman

Note by author: I'm really happy to say that since joining Bravo 22 I seem to have acquired a company of new tent pegs!

BEHIND

Behind my smile is a breaking heart,

Behind my laugh I'm falling apart.

Behind my eyes are tears at night,

Behind my body is a soul trying to fight.

Behind the face is a lack of hope,

Behind the strength I just can't cope.

Behind the walk I'm not quite home,

Behind the door I feel all alone.

Behind the jokes I think I can win,

Behind the lines I've got a devil within.

A Darker Shade of Blue

Behind the act I show as calm,

Behind the curtain I do self-harm.

Behind my actions I want to cry,

Behind the façade I feel I'm gonna die.

Behind the time is this the worse I get,

Behind the night I wake in cold sweat.

Behind my deeds you don't see,

Behind the day the devil inside me.

By Budgie Burgess

YOU'D NEVER GUESS...

Look at her with all that make-up

Look at her with all that plastic surgery

Look at her with all those tattoos

You'd never guess...

You'd never guess that she doesn't see what you do.

You'd never guess that she is horrified by what she sees in the mirror.

Look at her with her new hair do

Look at her with hardly's no make-up

Look at her with her toned down image

You'd never guess...

You'd never guess that she still can't understand why she looks so strange.

You'd never guess that she is still horrified by what she sees in the mirror.

A Darker Shade of Blue

Look at her smiling and laughing

Look at her doing everything she thought she couldn't

Look at her dealing with the demons

You'd never guess...

You'd never guess that she's faking it every single day.

You'd never guess that she does everything to avoid mirrors and reflective surfaces.

They call it body dysmorphia.

People say she's beautiful just the way she is.

People think she's just being silly.

You'd never guess what she really sees…

By Becky Rigg

UNTITLED

Mummy said you went to Jesus

She says that Daddy died

I'm too young to get all this

I want you by my side

You are my Daddy fixer man

You are my rugby coach

You pinched my chips from my plate

It's me who needs you most

I got all my spellings right

I'm learning about the sea

That was your favourite subject, other than me.

I know you're very proud of me

Of that theres no mistake

Mummy says you live in heaven now

I hope you have a good view

Please watch over me Daddy because I really love you

By Caroline Beer

JUST GOING TO THE SHOP

We need some milk

Go to the shop then

I can't

You can

I can't breathe

You'll be ok its not too far

I won't

You've done before and survived

I know but I feel dizzy today

You were dizzy last time and made it

Ok ok I'll go

Go put your shoes on then

Give give me a minute

Don't think about it just go

I know it's just not that easy though

You'll be okay though

Okay let's do it

I've got my shoes on

Get some money

Don't forget the keys

I've got everything

Let's go then

Right I'm going

I don't like this

It's gonna be fine be brave

I'm trying

I know

There's lots of people out

Don't worry about them

They will be able to tell and think I'm weird

Just focus on getting to the shop

Okay

We're nearly there

Let's be quick I don't like it

Go straight to the milk

I will

Then straight to the checkout

Oh god there's a queue

It's ok there's only one person

I can't do it let's go

You're here now

No no let's just go

Look you're next

Okay okay I can't breathe please hurry up

Go on it's your turn

Just this milk please

A pound please

There you go

Thank you

A Darker Shade of Blue

Thank you

See I told you could do it

Let's just go quickly

You're okay

I know I just want to get home

We're nearly there now that wasn't too bad

It was

We're here now see

Put the kettle on

Come on let's have a cup of tea

Okay then

By Colin Freeman

ALL ALONE

Emotionally drained I feel all alone

I still feel this even when all are home

But for the children I must stay strong

I may be doing good, but it feels all wrong

I lay in bed, think I'm gonna die

The wife sleeps next to me, it's then I cry

For the rest of the world my tears are unseen

I smile and laugh, but inside I scream

I feel I'm in a world of strangers

Always on edge, can't ignore the dangers

A Darker Shade of Blue

Thoughts, tastes and smells in my head

I've seen the hurt, I seen the dead

I've been to places, I've seen Hell

These are the thoughts I cannot tell

To live day to day, I have to take medication

I have to drink this my only sedation

I am on journey, I have come so far

I am getting treatment, thanks EMDR

This is my life, which most don't get to see

This is my life with PTSD

By Budgie Burgess

GUY FAWKES

It's getting close to the 5th of November

Please take a pause, please remember

You cheer and clap with delight

I curl up and hide, deep with fright

The rocket whoosh, and hit the sky

I hide in the corner, wanting to cry

You laugh and cheer at every sound

All I want to do, is hit the ground

You light the fire and put on the Guy

The noises make me pray, I don't wanna die

A Darker Shade of Blue

Throughout the night you have your fun

All I get is the smell and sound of a gun

So this fireworks please spare a thought

For those who have served, those who have fought

By Budgie Burgess

HOW I AM

This how I tell you, how I am
This is the best way, the only way I can

I put on a smile, day to day
The pain is deep, deeper than I could say

I may look ok, but I'm more than you see
I still get the voices that say, they gonna get me

I try to ignore them, but the deeper they gain
They want to cause me hurt, they want me in pain

I tell them they are not wanted, they are not real
But it's not how it is, it's not how I feel

I use the drink, and the meds to sleep
If I don't do this, I'm in the corner in a heap

A Darker Shade of Blue

I try to hide, I go to work
But even there, they seem to lurk

Is it the quiet, or is it through fear?
Should I cry, should I shed a tear?

If I did this, does it make me weak
If I do this, does the devil get my soul to keep

It's not just the voices, it's the thoughts in my head
The ones that tell me, I'm better off dead

I know it not true, they playing with my mind
I just need to keep going, then its peace I will find

I try to sleep, every moment a fight
It's then I'm filled with pain, I'm filled with fright

Scared to close my eyes, scared to sleep
Its then the devil gets me, gets my soul to keep

A Darker Shade of Blue

So at the moment and the pain so near,
I'll go to bed, in bed with fear

By Budgie Burgess

IS NO CURE

I'm not scared of the monsters under my bed

I'm scared of the monsters that are in my head

I'm haunted by ghosts and demons when I sleep

My unconsciousness awakens, what I buried so deep

It's what's in my mind, it's what I don't tell

These monsters and demons they come from hell

They cause me headaches, they go around my mind

Of thoughts and events, I want to leave behind

Some are like, get over it you'll be ok

Spend time in my head, a minute, hour or even a day

Then you hear the voices, and feel my pain

If you did this you would not be the same

Like the flu and much, much more

For PTSD there is no cure

Please stand by us, to the end

We all need someone on whom we can depend

With good friends and those we adore

We will get through this, we will win the war

By Budgie Burgess

LIFE WITH PTSD

I lie awake, I try to sleep

But into my mind they start to creep

To you it was news in a faraway land

For me it was war, a blooded hand

I try to relax, to just be normal

My regimented mind it is too formal

I want to just block it out, but it finds a way

To torment my mind, to spoil my day

The things I've seen, the things I've done

Should not be seen by anyone

A Darker Shade of Blue

I close my eyes and shut them tight

I'm frozen in terror, I'm frozen with fright

I re-live it again and it doesn't seem right

Why can't I sleep? Why must I fight?

It only takes a moment, a minute or so

A sight, a sound, a smell, and off I go

Not safe anymore though I am at home

Surrounded by people, but still feel alone

Someone's coming, coming to do me great harm

How do I keep safe? How to stay calm?

I'm up and I'm ready, 'Stood to' for the night

I know they're en-route, to win I will fight

A Darker Shade of Blue

Old sights and sounds are back once again

With the voices. They drive me insane

Although what is happening doesn't make sense

The slightest thing can cause me offence

"You're home and you're safe" is what people say

But they don't see the battles day to day

And then I am visited by an old friend

It's Death, he tells me "make it all end"

I tell them "No" and "Go away"

He looks and laughs, he is here to stay

I wonder how much I can take

My life right now, it seems so fake

A Darker Shade of Blue

I wave and smile and say I'm fine

But I'm falling deeper all the time

I can't always trust what I can hear or see

This is my battle, this is PTSD.

By Budgie Burgess

TELL MY WIFE

Just when I think I am doing so well

The thoughts come back, now I'm back in hell

I shout and punch things as I go by

I keep getting angry, and I don't know why

I want to live, be the best I can be

This anger and violence, this is not me

I need to stay strong, I need to be calm

This is not easy, the voices say self-harm

I want to laugh, I want to smile

It's been so long, it's been a while

A Darker Shade of Blue

I want it to stop, I want it to end

I should tell my wife, in her I can depend

What do I tell, what do I say

The last thing I want, is to ruin her day

I know she won't mind, I know this is right

I know she will stay with me, and help me fight

So how do I tell her, how to tell my wife

I want to live, I want a life

By Budgie Burgess

THE DEMONS IN THE MORNING

The Demons in the morning, I wake in fright

The Demons in the morning, the ones I fought at night

The Demons in the morning, the ones you don't see

The Demons in the morning, they hide within me

The Demons in the morning, they got me again

The Demons in the morning, they are driving me insane

The Demons in the morning, I must fight each day

The Demons in the morning, it's them I cannot say

The Demons in the morning, they are there when I wake

The Demons in the morning, my sole I must forsake

The Demons in the morning, it's that what I fear

The Demons in the morning, how do I make them disappear

The Demons in the morning, they tell what to think

The Demons in the morning, they tell me I must drink

The Demons in the morning, it's how I get by

The Demons in the morning, it's what makes me cry

The Demons in the morning, how long do they last

The Demons in the morning, keeps me in the past

The Demons in the morning, they are all I know

The Demons in the morning, I want to let go

The Demons in the morning, you are deeper than my skin

The Demons in the morning, I won't let you win

A Darker Shade of Blue

The Demons in the morning, this is the end

The Demons in the morning, I am on the mend

By Budgie Burgess

UNTITLED

I'm finding it hard, I'm starting to struggle

My minds all over, all in a muddle

Finding it hard to keep on task

I go to work, and put on a mask

I'm doing my best to keep calm

I'm doing it again, starting to self harm

I don't know when, I don't know why

I look at the marks, it makes me wanna cry

It's those voices going around my head

Tell me to hurt, say I'm better off dead

Is it to soothe me, is it a release

Is it the only way I will find peace

A Darker Shade of Blue

I sit there quiet, I don't want to talk

I thought I would be better after a walk

This did not help, I feel as bad

Am I going crazy, am I going mad

What can I do? I know it's all wrong

I feel I am always fighting, I am not that strong

I want to run away, I want to hide

But I can't get away from the demons inside

It gives me time, time to think

I still got meds, but need to drink

I need to rest, need to feel at ease

I ask for a beak, I beg you please

I know deep down it won't last

A Darker Shade of Blue

I know this as I survived the past

I will survive, and can be strong

I know deep down this won't last long

By Budgie Burgess

WALKING DEAD

How am I meant to feel
The dreams & pain seem so real

What am I meant to say
I feel all hope has gone away

When do I get a choice
All I hear is an endless voice

Flashbacks & vigilance abound
Peace and calm can't be found

Life is just passing me by
All I want is to cry

The Reaper, I see him a lot
I live in hell with the fight I've got

PTSD, I'm the walking dead
Stuck with voices & thoughts in my head

By Budgie Burgess

A JOURNEY WITH NO END

I am tired of walking this lonely street

Broken slabs and heavy feet

Head hanging low once again

Watching the water from into the drain

Just like me it is ebbing away

I have got to get through another day

I have got not reason to look up high

Just grey clouds that go floating by

No birds singing their joyful song

How did everything seem to go so wrong

Nothing there for me except a space

Inside my heart, no smile on my face

The tears start to fall in a silent stream

I hope that all this is just a horrible dream

It is better to have loved and lost is what they say

A Darker Shade of Blue

Stupid words as it is me they betray

But my head it lifts when the stars come out

The moonlight trying to wash away my doubt

But it envelops me and I am sinking lower

I am blind to its light and my it beats slower

By Tracey Ward

JUST ONE MORE

Just one more

Maybe two

Three is the

right amount

Four will surely do

Five might be pushing it

six what can go wrong?

The next thing I know

the packet is gone.

I eat to feel happiness

comfort and joy

Nothing cures

loneliness like a packet

of McCoys

when I am upset or

feeling quite glum

Sausage rolls and pizza

can be quite the thumbs

The feeling whilst eating

for me is pure bliss

like a warm loving hug or

a passionate kiss

If you want it so badly

just stop

Well that's absolutely

absurd

have you heard of an

addict give up with those words?

Sex, drugs, any addiction is hard

Anything can be

addicting, even spending

money, credit cards

On cigarette packets,

you get a clear warning

A picture of a tumour or

a family mourning

Deep fried snacks, crips

and takeaways are fine!

Don't worry about heart

disease or diabetes

It's not like it's the number one killer in

first world counties

A Darker Shade of Blue

It's advertised

everywhere, where've you go

Buy one get one free at

your nearest Tesco's

Social events, family do's,

restaurants, celebrations too

A delicious spread for all to see

I swear those chocolate fingers

are staring at me!

Imagine having to fight

your addiction everyday

It would be so much

easier to say

I'm quitting food altogether,

as from today!

A Darker Shade of Blue

You have such a pretty face

it's a shame you're that size

I laughed but deep down

it killed me inside

I try everyday

a better person I want to be

For myself, my health

and my family

I will keep on trying, but

addictions don't fray

I'll be fighting until my

very last day

We never know

what a person is thinking

Why they are smoking or why they are drinking

You never know what a persons been through

I have an addiction

I've shared it with you.

By Lilly Charles

BABY BLUES

You arrived, I left

You were fresh and new,

I was down and depressed

I couldn't hold you, feed you

I just turned my back

I was so scared of another anxiety attack

Such an amazing feeling I was told

to hold your new baby

a couple minutes old

A cold nasty darkness

took over my mind

Washing over my thoughts

and making me blind

A failure, a vile waste of space

Ashamed with myself

an utter disgrace

I stood in front of the

mirror one day,

I thought to myself

You should just go away!

You're nothing

a coward

no fitting mother

You're worthless, pointless

He deserves another

WAAAH!

Abruptly I ran to him

Once so agonising to see

he was my son and he

needed... ME!

With help from my

partner and family too

A Darker Shade of Blue

I started to feel less

down, less blue

It was gruelling,

strenuous but I made a start

Each giggle or hug, a

plaster to my shattered heart

I drowned out the

thoughts in my head

Replaced them with memories

family fun and stories in bed

Three years on and you're

growing up fast

A mop of curly hair, a

cheeky grin

My little monkey, my

everything

The love I feel now I

cannot describe

It's warm and so fuzzy

a positive vibe

A love for a child can not compare

You would not understand unless

you've been there.

By Lilly Charles

ANXIETY STRICKEN

Checked the door twice

Three times

I count in my head

Is it locked?

I think lying in bed.

Is the radiator still on?

Can I smell burning?

Is the clothing track too close?

My stomach starts churning.

My son is asleep

Can I feel his breath?

Don't leave food in his room

He might choke to death

A Darker Shade of Blue

Taking a shower all on my own

Eyes glued open

Never feeling alone

What if there's

someone hiding

Behind there, round the corner

On that shrouded chair

The darkness I

can't stand

or going out late,

A man with a knife

Deciding my fate

Social situations

Seeing new faces

A Darker Shade of Blue

Phone calls

visiting new places

Driving,

pressure

shopping and more

Things I find hard to do,

I really deplore

Childish fears,

you don't believe anymore

shadows, creaks,

footsteps, a tap on the door.

Gaps in the curtains at night

who's looking through?

Peaking through the crack

Just out of view

I forget what to do

I forget what I'm saying

Biting my nails and

constantly playing

With my hair, my clothes

and tapping my foot

I feel people stare, I hear them all tut

I stay up at night

Can't sleep from the fear,

That a burger or stranger

soon will appear

It makes me

second guess,

analyse everything I've

ever done wrong

Makes me agitated and angry

Lash out at loves ones.

When i do leave

the house

My mind is a jumble

A burning sensation

A niggling mumble

Did I make sure to lock it?

Are my keys in my pocket?

Will my socket explode

If I've left something on it?

Be careful when driving,

Please answer my call

For a second my mind

Sees you crash into a wall

I know it is silly,

And most thoughts

are fleeting,

But I still get that feeling

My heart heavily beating

For a genuine moment

My whole body tenses

This feeling of dread

Takes over my senses

Rapid heartbeat

Sweats, short of breath

Fits of crying and

feeling depressed.

In my head I know these

things shouldn't scare me

I try to be rational and try

to think clearly

But the feeling I get is

hard to describe

It's a little like stage fright

that flutter inside

That lump in your throat

A nagging frustrating sensation

A word or thought lost in

conversation.

What was that thing

you've forgotten to do?

That panic of loosing something

important to you

Mix it all together and

add a sinking feeling,

That is what I feel

that is how I am thinking.

By Lilly Charles

ALONE AT MIDNIGHT

12am … awake

1 am … awake

2 am —- awake

3 am … for goodness sake!

Tick, tick, tick tock

The sound of my

imaginary clock

A whisper of dreams

drifts from my right,

Where my partner sleeps

soundly all of the night

A Darker Shade of Blue

A silent frustration

Those demons decide

Clawing, scratching

scorching inside

They prod and

they poke,

They bite and they pick

The banging, the throbbing

As heavy as bricks

These hellish creatures

Play cruel little games

Depression, anxiety

Are some of their names

Sleep I can not

A Darker Shade of Blue

Until sun light

glares through

For some reason

The beams disintegrate you

Exhausted I close

my eyes

I'm starting to sink

The land of nod

draws closer

Every exhausted blink

Good morning mummy

I wipe the stardust away

My little one has awoken

And wants me to play

I ache and i moan

Though just twenty three

I rattle and groan

As I make breakfast tea

Another bad night?

I am asked patiently

A blanket of love

Comes to rescue me

During the day

Busy and bustling

Toddler antics

Housework and dusting

Soon it's that time again

The world is asleep

I'm lying in bed

On my two

hundredth sheep

A gut wrenching churn

In the pit of my soul

Exhausted of fighting

It's taking its toll.

12 am … awake

1am … awake

2 am … awake

3 am … for goodness sake!

By Lilly Charles

A CHARITABLE MIND

My thoughts are a shape,

before the dissipation of my words.

My works do not reach the outer limits of my soul.

So do large structures fall down, and green grass becomes softly grazed.

The house is empty.

This soul, which shines as flame behind glass, has been manufactured.

Its light wavers, before the flood.

My head is a sphere within an egg, or an autumnal summer.

I consider everything I try to be loveless

Kind words are not enough, from this upshot of the rind.

This seed trickles down the bumpy cobbles, all engulfed.

At least those others are not perturbed by a warm smile.

They used to be, because the smile once sealed a broken heart.

Our thoughts were like the wispy October haze.

The pane of warped glass was within the rotting frame.

No longer could we connect, and love had been lost behind numbers and spans.

Mist clouded the window, and it could never be fully cleared.

Mine is not a charitable mind.

My bright gaze is tired, and I do not see through the pane to the other world.

My love is a reflection, and doesn't unlock your heart.

Mist clouds the surface of the window, and you haven't scratched it yet.

By John Mullen

THE JAR BY THE RIVER

I found a glass jar, by the winding river, and found a strange letter inside.

Then I walked to a nearby village, before I rested near an ancient shrine.

At the end of the letter, dampened and blurred, an even stranger note was at the end.

In blue, the numbers 193345 were from the anonymous writer's pen.

My friend once worked, in a glass factory, and had done so for over 3 years.

Her hand was once burned, by the molten glass, and her vision became impaired.

Her doctor, from number 45, was a Ghanaian.

We met at the pub until late.

He said to me, that his blue wrist-watch, read twenty-seven minutes to eight.

The doctor, whom I thanked, once fished in the Volta before God decided his fate.

That the gun-laden forces would make his family hostage, and with twelve others he was to emigrate.

Crammed in a large dingy, in the sun baked ocean, they had one jar of food left to share.

The doctor wrote his phone number, to put in the jar, with the torn-vest crew in despair.

When they prayed for whoever opened the jar, and the letter, their hands were loyally secure.

Then the doctor's eyes set on, a white light on the horizon.

A floating haven they couldn't be sure?

I bought a diamond ring, for my friends healed hand, with the reward received from the hearing.

On her 33rd birthday, by the reeds in the river, we were wedded with others rejoicing.

Many folks tell, this strange story of the jar, will mean the doctor and his long-lost embrace.

He will meet other survivors, and this letter should remind us, of ruptures in our cold fallen race.

By John Mullen

FAITH, BELIEF WITHOUT EVIDENCE

I thought I'd lived my hardest times when my husband died but I kept my faith

Bringing up two children, making ends meet, was hard at times, but I kept my faith.

One awful day my beautiful daughter lost her mind but I kept my faith.

She wanted to attack me, she thought I was a witch, but I kept my faith.

I tried to get close to her, she wouldn't let me, it broke my heart, but I kept my faith.

i spent night after night crying, unable to sleep, worried sick, but I kept my faith.

She got better, i thought it was over, it all happened again, psychosis, but I kept my faith.

I felt people judged me, judged my family, thought it was us, but I kept my faith.

They looked into every aspect of our lives, I felt interrogated , but I kept my faith.

My daughter was pinned down, put in seclusion, held like a prisoner, but I kept my faith.

I knew the family had to be at their best, some had therapy, a long eight months, but I kept my faith.

I grew strength I didn't know I had, to face each day and every day, I kept my faith.

I deducted every possible moment I could to help her come back, I kept my faith.

I realised that it wasn't them vs me it was united for Marie, I kept my faith.

I gathered as much information as I could, I realise I needed to take time for me, I kept my faith.

I realised there is a bigger picture, I had to trust whatever would happen, I kept my faith.

I learnt the strongest trees, grow in the strongest winds not the best soil, I kept my faith.

When I couldn't be there, I knew we were energetically connected, so I kept my faith.

I learnt that this is earth school, there are tests, lessons and big exams, I kept my faith.

I choose to see even the darkest things with unconditional love, I ket my faith.

I learnt patience and more understanding than I ever had, I taught it to her, I kept her faith.

We did evert possible empowerment exercise, yoga and all, we kept our faith.

We held visions of a better future, we did guided meditations, we kept our faith.

I understood it was no one's fault, in a world of blame love is the answer, I kept my faith.

Life is full of lessons, learn them all, do your best, pray when you can, keep your faith.

Seeing Marie so well, happy, smiling and back in the game makes me feel blessed, thank you faith.

Faith can be in yourself, in the doctors, in the master plan or in God itself, keep your faith.

Life was not meant to be a fairy tale, we grow the most from the hard times we face, if you keep your faith.

Whatever life throws your way, spring always follows winter, joy will came again, if you keep your faith.

I am grateful to the Doctors and everybody here, my daughter is better and you re-enforced my faith.

I will be forever thankful for the love and care beyond your duties, thank you for YOUR faith.

By Anon

IF ONLY

It's ok don't look

It's ok to not be ok

Just don't drain me

And talking is good just not too much

It's getting old

Should you not be ok by now

That's ok

Avoid opening the message

Look down don't ask

How are you not again

Who can blame you

I would not want to know either

I wont someone else can

Yes someone not me

Some joke

But I have a sense of humour

So look fed up of hearing it

A Darker Shade of Blue

Some pity but no one understands

And talking never changes things

The same responses

One day at a time; baby steps

You are worthy

All words and only words of empathy

From caring souls who have pain too

But how can words fix broken minds hearts

And believe what is broken some times can not be fixed

And some fights have winners and losers this fight cant last
forever

Michael Fenton

ME

They say you have to love your self but who am I?

I want to be me but I'm emotional and get hurt so easy

I don't like me

I don't like feelings

I wish I could close the door on them

The helpless feeling

Of not being able to fix the hurt of others

The feeling of not being complete

The fear of never knowing if I will be in control

I want to love me but me is a man

Who loves too much and wants to feel happiness

In a world of pain the world is a harsh cruel place

And only the strongest move forward

I want to be a better person

But how do I change and become cold and emotionally void

It's the me the world has asked for

Safe from hurt and pain

But also untrusting and mean

Or do I accept who I am and hope that there is more in this world

More then I have seen

The joys life brings are real

But the knowledge of how it can all come crashing down are real

I wish it was not so but life's game does not play fair

And we live outside of happy ever after

Do we have the ability to change our world?

Or is fate; a force like gravity

I don't know any more

Over thinking, under living

Joy turns to fear

Pride to pity if I can't control my mind

Can I close the heart

But something has to give

If I am forced to play this game

Then let me be the player in control of my moves

A Darker Shade of Blue

And stop changing the rules

Let me wipe the memories away

So I can see a future

Not an empty world of old age and pain

Is it me who has control

No I just have to decide

Who I am but love him as well

I can't love either any more

One is weak and one is empty

And I can't be any more

So who am I?

I am lost

I give my all

Now I am just required to survive

For the only love I have left

Please don't take this away next like everything else

And don't take me from them

Even if I beg for it

I will keep going as a shell and pretend for them

ME continued…

By Michael Fenton

THE FIRST MOMENT

I can not tell you when I fist felt the darkness

Or why

But I can tell you it's not always the same

It's not always wanting to die

And yes I did hate myself that much

But also about not wanting to live

You don't actively look for ways to make it happen

But you would not step out the way if it came

You may see good ways

The family would be well looked after

If it was the pissed judge

Who is let off by the county bobby who hit me

I would not avoid that accident

And it deals with the all too troublesome problem life!

But as long as I can remember

It was there in some form

Whether in the smallest corner of my mind

A Darker Shade of Blue

Always dulling the colours of my memory

Or at the front of my brain

In the middle of the storms

It's there

The first moment was like a light switch

And an accident

I was positive and thinking of life quotes

Cross roads and turning back

So you find a happy place

And there it was happy

I don't want to die with out feeling

It's one more real happiness

I don't want to miss it

The world was somehow brighter then before

Would it last I don't know

But it was there and real

And I hold it now so I will never forget

By Michael Fenton

LEAVE ME

It's not easy to not see you

I have tried not to look

But you pop up all the times that I try to avoid

But there you are and I'm invisible

I see smiles and love from the cold that I block

But every memory that has a comment

There you are smiling back at me

I now push further away from the world

With the darkness that has always been there

Because the light has gone

But I never deserved it any way

By Michael Fenton

PROMISE

I intend and I fight every day

But the longing is hard

I will fight but I wish

This pain is so hard and I still fight

I love still but it's not the same

I promise and I will always remember

But if I fail please don't think I forgot

Please don't think I wanted to break it

But I was weak

I was lost

And I can't help it

It's got me and it wont let go

I will always love you

But this is a hell I can't escape

My failure is my weakness

And I was not good enough

To save you from my hell

A Darker Shade of Blue

I never wanted to pass the pain

But I failed

By Michael Fenton

IT'S NOT GOOD TO TALK PARANOIA

Talk no I did and it helped for a while

It took some of the shame away

But if you do hurry

And get better sooner

Because later it gets old

And people stop asking

Avoid eye contact

But at least they have stopped with the one line words of wisdom

With a soft hurt look

Sorry baby steps

I'm 5'9" would a stride back to sanity be wise?

One day at a time

You mean I cant skip Monday to Friday?

And have an extra weekend boooo lol

But it's ok they now know your mind is broken

So cutting you off is ok someone else will talk to you

Maybe Mavis in the butty shop

Or go see Jeff in the workshop

He loves a joke about your twitch wink for the boy eh

Just remember everybody is hiding their own battles

Check you phone the eight people you have asked how's your day?

They may have responded

No not opened

I'm sure it's not glued to their hand

Like to 23 people in this office

But I'm sure they're all good !

By Michael Fenton

BI-POLAR - BARE

As my time piece does. Clock the watching wall,

Daring all hours and mins to catch me by,

I match my cig desire at this roll call,

To fire my thought in drag from polar's high.

So cajole's blague winds in my troubled mind

And wraps in doles of careless kind of talk,

Wherein I stalk in id's subconscious bind,

To dork in a delusion's trance like walk.

Yet in cognisant's strike do I now dwell,

In deep emotions swell of confused thoughts

Where manic courts can't in obsession's hell,

And moments of awareness flick contort's.

So as I rate in polar as I be

Then mate in stress is in my mind I see !

By Barry Bradshaigh

LIVING WITH PTSD, A POEM BY A WIFE

Sometimes I want to run away
Feel I can't take another day
I'm off my meds, so am I mad?
Or is life really getting bad?

I feel ok, I feel quite 'sane'
But is my mood on the turn again?
The air is thick with words unsaid
I want to go and hide in my bed

He signs, he swears, he looks so sad
I smile, laugh, so it seems less bad
The kids look tense
I walk on egg shells in defence

It's so exhausting doing this
Crawling through the dark abyss
It's such hard work to just keep swimming
I'm terrified my mood is dipping

I can't afford to get so low
It would become a double blow
If I give in then what would happen?
Our fragile life would soon be cracking

And so I plod, one foot then another
After all I am a mother
I can't give up, I sure can't stop
And to be fair I wouldn't swap

It may be hard, it may cause pain
But in the end, happiness I'll claim

By Anonymous

THE BLACKBIRD OF ST. THOMAS'

At three o'clock this morning
I went to find the blackbird
who is always singing whenever I'm walking
home over Westminster Bridge

I found him down in the hospital grounds
perched by the fountain in a leafless tree
proud in black with head thrown back
against the huge white moon of Big Ben

 "How come you always sing so sweet?" I asked
"so many hours from dawn?"

and in a voice flushed with pride
he told me that this was his calling
to serenade the newborns
lying naked behind the windows of North Wing

so that whenever these children are lost
in the darkness of a concrete world
deep in their hearts they will always know
the song of the joy of Spring.

By Ian Longstaff

DREAMS OF BELONGING

i)

I have just returned
from somewhere quite strange.

A collection
of ramshackle houses
sitting on daisy-dotted lawns
ringed by pallet-wood fences

roofs scaled with hubcaps
rescued from lonely roadsides
their faces to the sun

and when it rains
the drip-drops drip
into jam jars dangling
waiting to be
whistled into tea

brews to wash down
wedges of cake
lovingly served
on crackledy plates
and devoured
using runaway teaspoons.

ii)

Nearly every night it seems
there's dancing

at the village hall

everyone going crazy
in their stockinged feet

stomping and whooping
to the one-string fiddles
and the dented horns
of the Broken Instrument Band

and as evening wanes
danced-out, odd-socked feet are reunited
with their found on motorway trainers

and half-asleep children
are carried, limbs lolling
strange silhouettes
that melt
into the night.

iii)

It's kind of funny (but kinda cool)
how nothing here really goes
and yet everything just seems to fit!

Like the faces smiling back at me.
I realise that, although I don't know anybody
I feel like I know every body

and I'm sure that
if I ever need a hand
with my tumbledown shack

I'd be swamped
by waves of neighbours

wearing holes for cardigans
and cheerily fixing
everything in sight
with hand-worn tools
from the sheds
of long-lost Granddads.

iv)

We are all here:

the odd
the awkward
the last to be picked
the somehow passed by
the never quite understood

stray dogs
and lost souls

square pegs
for once

in square holes.

By Ian Longstaff

BETTER DAYS ARE COMING

It's okay for you to sit and cry,
To shout and scream,
To close your eyes and dream.
Wish of times when the world didn't seem so blue,
Awash with tears, drowning in fear.
It's okay if you feel lost and confused,
Your energy dwindling, your soul so bruised.
It's okay if most days you want to give in, to the sadness and darkness that comes from within.
It's okay to feel however you feel, your thoughts are all valid, there's no need to conceal.
There's no right or wrong way when it comes to surviving, just keep faith that better days will come and we're still trying.
To keep hold of our loved ones, and protect them with all our might, if love alone could build sunbeams then we'd never see the night.
Just try and remember all the things you accomplish too cos getting up and facing it all isn't always the easiest to do.

by Niki Wilde (Thomas)

A Darker Shade of Blue

Chapter 2

Mental Health Assessments You Can Take

How have you been feeling lately?

When it comes to emotions, it can sometimes be hard to recognise or admit that we're not feeling 100%.

If you are 16 or over, take any of these short questionnaires to:

- Help you better understand how you've been feeling over the last 2 weeks

- Point you in the right direction for helpful advice and information

If you are struggling, the self assessment links below are not intended to replace a consultation with a GP. Please make an appointment with your doctors surgery; you can also print them off and take them with you to your appointment so you can go through them in more detail or feel embarrassed or difficulty expressing how you feel.

https://www.nhs.uk/conditions/stress-anxiety-depression/mood-self-assessment/

https://screening.mhanational.org/screening-tools

https://www.psychologytoday.com/gb/tests/health/mental-health-assessment

https://www.time-to-change.org.uk/mental-health-quiz

For anyone under 16 there is a brilliant website you can visit called:

https://youngminds.org.uk/find-help/feelings-and-symptoms/

A Darker Shade of Blue

Chapter 3

A-Z How And Where To Get Help

When to seek professional help

If support from family and friends and positive lifestyle changes aren't enough, it may be time to seek help from a mental health professional. There are many effective treatments for depression, including:

Therapy

Effective treatment for depression often includes consulting a therapist who can provide you tools to treat depression from a variety of angles and motivate you to take the action necessary. Therapy can also offer you the skills and insight to prevent depression from coming back.

Medication

Medication may be imperative if you're feeling suicidal or violent. But while it can help relieve symptoms of depression in some people, it isn't a cure and is not usually a long-term solution. It also comes with side effects and other drawbacks so it's important to learn all the facts to make an informed decision.

A to Z

Anxiety UK

Charity providing support if you have been diagnosed with an anxiety condition.

Phone: 03444 775 774 (Monday to Friday, 9.30am to 5.30pm)

Website: www.anxietyuk.org.uk

Bipolar UK

A charity helping people living with manic depression or bipolar disorder.

Website: www.bipolaruk.org.uk

CALM

CALM is the Campaign Against Living Miserably, for men aged 15 to 35.

Phone: 0800 58 58 58 (daily, 5pm to midnight)

Website: www.thecalmzone.net

Men's Health Forum

24/7 stress support for men by text, chat and email.

Website: www.menshealthforum.org.uk

Mental Health Foundation

Provides information and support for anyone with mental health problems or learning disabilities.

Website: www.mentalhealth.org.uk

Mind

Promotes the views and needs of people with mental health problems.

Phone: 0300 123 3393 (Monday to Friday, 9am to 6pm)

Website: www.mind.org.uk

No Panic

Voluntary charity offering support for sufferers of panic attacks and obsessive compulsive disorder (OCD). Offers a course to help overcome your phobia or OCD.

Phone: 0844 967 4848 (daily, 10am to 10pm). Calls cost 5p per minute plus your phone provider's Access Charge

Website: www.nopanic.org.uk

OCD Action

Support for people with OCD. Includes information on treatment and online resources.

Phone: 0845 390 6232 (Monday to Friday, 9.30am to 5pm). Calls cost 5p per minute plus your phone provider's Access Charge

Website: www.ocdaction.org.uk

OCD UK

A charity run by people with OCD, for people with OCD. Includes facts, news and treatments.

Phone: 0333 212 7890 (Monday to Friday, 9am to 5pm)

Website: www.ocduk.org

PAPYRUS

Young suicide prevention society.

Phone: HOPElineUK 0800 068 4141 (Monday to Friday, 10am to 5pm and 7pm to 10pm, and 2pm to 5pm on weekends)

Website: www.papyrus-uk.org

Rethink Mental Illness

Support and advice for people living with mental illness.

Phone: 0300 5000 927 (Monday to Friday, 9.30am to 4pm)

Website: www.rethink.org

Samaritans

Confidential support for people experiencing feelings of distress or despair.

Phone: 116 123 (free 24-hour helpline)

Website: www.samaritans.org.uk

SANE

Emotional support, information and guidance for people affected by mental illness, their families and carers.

Textcare: comfort and care via text message, sent when the person needs it most: www.sane.org.uk/textcare

Peer support forum: www.sane.org.uk/supportforum

Website: www.sane.org.uk/support

YoungMinds

Information on child and adolescent mental health. Services for parents and professionals.

Phone: Parents' helpline 0808 802 5544 (Monday to Friday, 9.30am to 4pm)

Website: www.youngminds.org.uk

Abuse (child, sexual, domestic violence)

NSPCC

Children's charity dedicated to ending child abuse and child cruelty.

Phone: 0800 1111 for Childline for children (24-hour helpline)

0808 800 5000 for adults concerned about a child (24-hour helpline)

Website: www.nspcc.org.uk

Refuge

Advice on dealing with domestic violence.

Phone: 0808 2000 247 (24-hour helpline)

Website: www.refuge.org.uk

Alcohol misuse

Alcoholics Anonymous

A free self-help group. Its "12 step" programme involves getting sober with the help of regular face-to-face and online support groups.

Phone: 0800 917 7650 (24-hour helpline)

Website: www.alcoholics-anonymous.org.uk

Al-Anon

Al-Anon is a free self-help "12 step" group for anyone whose life is or has been affected by someone else's drinking

Phone: 0800 0086 811 (daily, 10am to 10pm)

Website: https://www.al-anonuk.org.uk/

Drinkline

A free confidential helpline for people worried about their own or someone else's drinking.

Phone: 0300 123 1110 (weekdays 9am to 8pm, weekends 11am to 4pm)

National Association for Children of Alcoholics

National Association for Children of Alcoholics offers free confidential advice and information to everyone affected by a parent's drinking including children, adults and professionals.

Phone: 0800 358 3456 (Friday, Saturday and Monday 12pm to 7pm and Tuesday, Wednesday and Thursday 12pm to 9pm)

Website: https://www.nacoa.org.uk/

SMART Recovery UK

SMART Recovery UK face-to-face and online groups help people decide whether they have a problem with alcohol and drugs, build up their motivation to change, and offer a set of proven tools and techniques to support recovery.

Phone: 0330 053 6022 for general enquiries about SMART Recovery UK (9am to 5pm, Monday-Friday)

Website: https://smartrecovery.org.uk/

Alzheimer's

Alzheimer's Society

Provides information on dementia, including factsheets and helplines.

Phone: 0300 222 1122 (Monday to Friday, 9am to 5pm and 10am to 4pm on weekends)

Website: www.alzheimers.org.uk

Bereavement

Cruse Bereavement Care

Phone: 0808 808 1677 (Monday to Friday, 9am to 5pm)

Website: www.cruse.org.uk

Crime victims

Rape Crisis

To find your local services phone: 0808 802 9999 (daily, 12pm to 2.30pm and 7pm to 9.30pm)

Website: www.rapecrisis.org.uk

Victim Support

Phone: 0808 168 9111 (24-hour helpline)

Website: www.victimsupport.org

Drug misuse

Cocaine Anonymous

A free self-help group. Its "12 step" programme involves stopping using cocaine and all other mind-altering substances with the help of regular face-to-face and online support groups.

Phone: 0800 612 0225 (daily, 10am to 10pm)

Website: https://cocaineanonymous.org.uk/

FRANK

Free, confidential information and advice about drugs, their effects and the law. FRANK's live chat service runs daily from 2pm to 6pm.

Phone: 0300 1236600 (24-hour helpline)

Text a question to: 82111

Website: https://www.talktofrank.com/

Marijuana Anonymous

A free self-help group. Its "12 step" programme involves stopping using marijuana with the help of regular face-to-face and online support groups.

Phone: 0300 124 0373 (callback service)

Website: http://www.marijuana-anonymous.org.uk/

Narcotics Anonymous

A free self-help group. Its "12 step" programme involves stopping using drugs with the help of regular face-to-face and online support groups.

Phone: 0300 999 1212 (daily, 10am to midnight)

Website: www.ukna.org

SMART Recovery UK

SMART Recovery UK face-to-face and online groups help people decide whether they have a problem with alcohol and drugs, build up their motivation to change, and offer a set of proven tools and techniques to support recovery.

Phone: 0330 053 6022 for general enquiries about SMART Recovery UK (9am to 5pm, Monday-Friday)

Website: https://smartrecovery.org.uk/

Eating disorders

B-eat

Phone: 0808 801 0677 (adults) or 0808 801 0711 (for under-18s)

Website: www.b-eat.co.uk

Gambling

Gamblers Anonymous

A free self-help group. Its "12 step" programme involves stopping gambling with the help of regular face-to-face and online support groups.

Phone: 0330 094 0322 (24-hour)

Website: https://www.gamblersanonymous.org.uk/

Gam-Anon

A free self-help group. Its "12 step" programme is for those affected by someone else's gambling with the help of regular face-to-face and online support groups.

Phone: 08700 50 88 80

Website: www.gamanon.org.uk

National Gambling Helpline

Phone: 0808 8020 133 (daily, 8am to midnight)

Website: www.begambleaware.org

National Problem Gambling Clinic

A specialist NHS clinic for problem gamblers aged 13 and over.

Phone: 020 7381 7722 (callback)

Website: https://www.cnwl.nhs.uk/services/mental-health-services/addictions-and-substance-misuse/national-problem-gambling-clinic

Learning disabilities

Mencap

Charity working with people with a learning disability, their families and carers.

Phone: 0808 808 1111 (Monday to Friday, 9am to 5pm)

Website: www.mencap.org.uk

Parenting

Family Lives

Advice on all aspects of parenting, including dealing with bullying.

Phone: 0808 800 2222 (Monday to Friday, 9am to 9pm and Saturday to Sunday, 10am to 3pm)

Website: www.familylives.org.uk

Relationships

Relate

The UK's largest provider of relationship support.

Website: www.relate.org.uk

Headspace

https://www.headspace.com

NHS

https://www.nhs.uk/oneyou/every-mind-matters/coping-loneliness-during-coronavirus-outbreak/

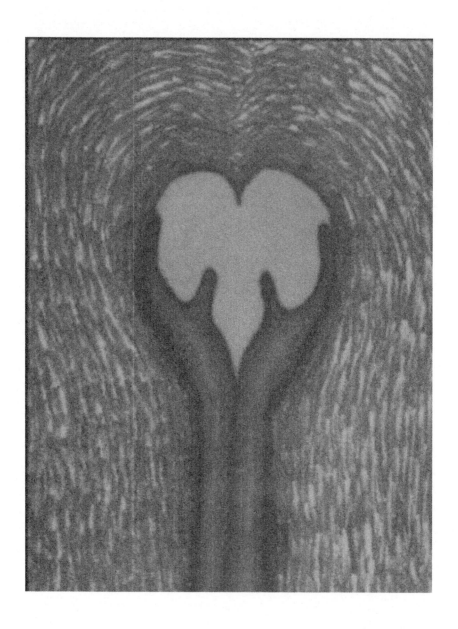

Chapter 4

Complementary Therapies and Depression

What are Complementary Therapies and how do they work

Complementary and alternative therapies typically take a holistic approach to your physical and mental health. This means that they consider all aspects of your physical and emotional wellbeing as a whole, rather than treating particular symptoms separately. For example, some complementary therapies focus on the mind, body and spirit or on the flow of energy through your body.

Many of these approaches have roots in ancient Eastern philosophies of health or the kinds of traditional healing methods used widely before the development of the treatment models currently used by the NHS.

Why might I try them?

There are many reasons you might decide to try complementary or alternative therapies. For example:

- You don't want the treatment your doctor has offered (such as psychiatric medication or talking therapies).

- You've already tried the treatments your doctor has offered and they haven't suited you (for example, you haven't found a psychiatric medication that works, or it's caused unwanted side effects).

- You're on an NHS waiting list for treatment, but you need help to manage your symptoms right away.

- You want more options to try in addition to the treatments your doctor has offered.

- You don't agree with your doctor's approach and you want to take another approach to looking after your mental health.

Can they treat mental health problems?

Complementary and alternative therapies can be used as a treatment for both physical and mental health problems. The particular problems that they can help will depend on the specific therapy that you are interested in, but many can help to reduce feelings of depression and anxiety. Some people also find they can help with sleep problems, relaxation and feelings of stress.

Guided meditation

There are various different schools of meditation, but all aim to quieten your mind and put you into a state of calm, stillness and rest. Some types of meditation may also involve mindfulness.

While the evidence is mixed as to whether meditation is effective at treating mental health problems, many people do find it a helpful way of relaxing and managing feelings of stress and anxiety.

What are the hormonal and cellular effects of meditation?

Both guided meditation and deep relaxation have a number of amazing effects on your body and hormones.

- Meditation slows down brain wave activity and subdues stress all the while triggering human growth hormones (HGH) . HGH helps regulate your metabolism, stimulate fat cells to reduce the amount of stored fats, promote protein synthesis in cells, and play a role in regulating your blood sugar.

- Meditation helps calm the adrenals and allow them to rest, relieving them from over-producing cortisol — the stress hormone — which has a devastating effect on your thyroid function and the ability to lose weight.

- Meditation takes your endocrine system out of a state of high alert. Hormonal secretion becomes regulated and all of your hormonal systems — thyroid, adrenals, sex hormones etc — have an opportunity to come back into balance and restore your soul.

- Both meditation and relaxation allow your body to truly rests, and that's when you restore balance and renew vitality throughout your entire body. That is not always the case with sleep. Meditation also improves the quality of your sleep as it quells the endless chatter of your mind.

- Meditation alkalises your system, balancing out acidity that has accrued through the overactivity of your analytical mind and the fear-based thinking that generates stress hormones.

- Meditation decreases inflammation at the cellular level neutralising acidosis and minimising pain.

You can find guided meditations on my blog page https://traceyward.me

Mindfulness

Mindfulness involves focusing your attention to what's happening in the present moment. It aims to help you become more aware of your thoughts and feelings, so you can choose how to react to them calmly.

Many people find mindfulness helpful for managing negative thoughts and feelings of stress.

Mindfulness improves well-being

Increasing your capacity for mindfulness supports many attitudes that contribute to a satisfied life. Being mindful makes it easier to savor the pleasures in life as they occur, helps you become fully engaged in activities, and creates a greater capacity to deal with adverse events. By focusing on the here and now, many people who practice mindfulness find that they are less likely to get caught up in worries about the future or regrets over the past, are less preoccupied with concerns about success and self-esteem, and are better able to form deep connections with others.

Mindfulness improves physical health

If greater well-being isn't enough of an incentive, scientists have discovered that mindfulness techniques help improve physical health in a number of ways. Mindfulness can: help relieve stress, treat heart disease, lower blood pressure, reduce chronic pain, , improve sleep, and alleviate gastrointestinal difficulties.

Mindfulness improves mental health

In recent years, psychotherapists have turned to mindfulness meditation as an important element in the treatment of a number of problems, including: depression, substance abuse, eating disorders, couples' conflicts, anxiety disorders, and obsessive-compulsive disorder

Aromatherapy and massage

Aromatherapy uses essential oils (oils extracted from plants) for healing. Some people find that the smell (aroma) of particular oils helps them to relax, sleep better, relieve pain and improve low mood. For example, when used appropriately lavender and chamomile essential oils are thought to be relaxing and help you sleep.

The oils can be used in many different ways, such as in creams, oil burners, massaged into the skin or by adding drops to a warm bath.

It is possible to experience allergies or reactions to the oils, so you should speak to an aromatherapist beforehand if you have any concerns.

What to expect?

Feeling burnt out? If you've been running on empty, an aromatherapy massage could be just what you need to recharge your batteries. Massages are usually pretty relaxing, but it's the addition of essential oils (the aromatherapy part) that makes this treatment truly transformative. Essential oils can do everything from energising to de-stress or reinvigorate, so your therapist will have a proper consultation with you before you start to assess where you're at emotionally, as well as checking in on any aches and pains. From there, your therapist can create exactly the right blend of essential oils (plus something called a 'carrier' oil, which stops the super-potent essential oils irritating your skin) for your needs and your massage can begin.

How does it work?

The power of essential oils is twofold. Firstly, through inhalation, you'll be relaxed by their lovely calming smell, but also, they penetrate the skin and move quickly into your bloodstream, loosening any muscle pains and working on any suppressed tension you've got. Through the physical effects of the oil on your body, and the smells travelling through your super-sensitive nasal passage to your brain to help relax you emotionally, you can imagine why some people manage to totally conk out during an aromatherapy massage.

After an hour to an hour and a half, you'll be ready to drift on out – despite how much you might not want to. All those oils can be (conversely) a little dehydrating internally, so make sure to drink plenty of water afterwards to keep your hydration levels topped up.

Good to know

Aromatherapy massage can be particularly good for sleep problems, persistent period pains, digestive woes and eczema, but it's not usually advised in pregnancy or for anyone with kidney problems, due to the potency of the essential oils.

Reflexology

Reflexology is based on the idea that different points on your feet, hands, face and ears are linked to other parts of your body through your nervous system. During a typical session, a reflexologist will use their hands to apply gentle pressure to these points.

Reflexologists recommend this treatment as a way to relieve tension, improve mood and help you to sleep.

By applying healing energy to specific areas on your feet – known as reflexes – reflexology sends signals through the body which, in turn, release positive chemicals, like endorphins. The result? Reduced stress and pain. The treatment is also said to decrease toxins and increase blood supply, easing tension and inflammation.

And with thousands of nerves in each foot alone, it's a real skill to know exactly where to touch! Therapists use reflexology maps, which enable them to see which specific part of the foot relates to different areas of the body's nervous system. Take your toes for example, that correspond directly to your head. Or your lower back and intestines, and their link to your heel. That's why the goal is to relax not just your feet, but your entire body from tip to toe.

Is it for me?

If you're a bit squeamish about having your feet touched, fear not. You can have the exact same treatment on your hands if you prefer. Reflexology can help ease conditions including arthritis, headaches, migraines, PMS and even fertility issues. Plus, the number of sessions you choose to have is entirely up to you. Many people find themselves feeling healthier and more energetic after just a few. So if you're sore, stressed out or simply run down, give reflexology a go

Reiki

Reiki is a Japanese technique that involves the 'laying of hands' on different areas of the body including the head, shoulders, stomach and feet. It's based on the idea that we have a 'life force energy' that flows within our bodies. When this energy is low, it makes us more likely to become unwell.

A Reiki treatment aims to restore life force energy to help you to heal and stay well. Some people find it makes them feel more relaxed and less stressed.

Swedish massage

Massage uses touch in a sensitive and respectful way, taking account of physical symptoms, wellbeing, and your lifestyle. There are lots of different types of massage therapy, such as Shiatsu, Indian head massage and aromatherapy massage.

What is Swedish massage good for?

The various Swedish massage techniques are designed to improve your circulation, soothe your muscles and make you feel more relaxed.

Swedish massage uses softer strokes on the bonier and more delicate parts of the body, and stronger strokes where there is thicker muscle coverage. This adjustment of pressure makes it an ideal massage for relaxation.

Besides the calming benefits, Swedish massage is thought to be good for:

- easing muscular strain by flushing out toxins

- improving circulation by increasing the oxygen flow in the blood

- helping to keep ligaments and tendons supple

- reducing emotional and physical stress.

Yoga Laughter

The benefits of laughter

Laughter Club sessions relieve stress, boosts immunity, fights depression, and eventually make people into more positive thinkers.

When you start laughing, your chemistry changes, your physiology changes, your chances to experience happiness are much greater. A Karma Times Laughter Club session is nothing more than prepping the body and mind for happiness.

The sources of laughter

Laughter has two sources, one from the body, one from the mind. Adults tend to laugh from the mind. We use judgments and evaluations about what's funny and what isn't. Children, who laugh much more frequently than adults, laugh from the body. They laugh all the time they're playing. Taking part in a Karma Times Laughter Club session is based on cultivating your childlike playfulness. We all have a child inside us wanting to laugh, wanting to play.

William Fry, a psychiatrist at Stanford University states that in a career that spanned more than 50 years, he documented some of the health benefits of what he calls "mirthful laughter." In a series of studies, Fry and his colleagues found that laughter increases circulation, stimulates the immune system, exercises the muscles, and even invigorates the brain. Other researchers have found that laughter reduces stress hormones and may even help prevent heart disease.

What about fake laughter?

But can fake laughter—laughter devoid of humour, laughter that's forced rather than spontaneous—have the same beneficial effects? Fry believes that aside from the mental stimulation that comes in the moment of discovery when you hear a good joke or appreciate a pun, the effects should be largely the same. "I think it's definitely beneficial," says Fry and "I'm very much in favour of this".

What happens at a Karma Times yoga laughter session

We start with a standard warm-up and some deep breathing before moving onto the laughter exercises. To begin with, it is completely normal to feel a bit stupid but I promise it will not last very long. So do not worry if the laughter feels forced. If you can't laugh; fake it.

The body doesn't know the difference between real laughter and fake laughter. All sessions will include a guided meditation at the end of the session. You can find yoga laughter clubs all over the world.

A Darker Shade of Blue

Chapter 5

Change Your Life Today And Become A Better Version Of Yourself

I came to the conclusion while writing this book that it is no good just tackling one aspect of your life. Your life consists of different components. You are like a jigsaw puzzle and we need to get all those pieces together and in the right place. I once described myself as a very old iPhone. I had all the right apps i.e. knowledge, dedication, courage, health, exercise, sleep patterns, diet but of a very old phone etc but I needed a huge software update to get them up to speed and working properly and with each other and this is what this chapter will be summarising.

Sleep

The first thing I want to go through is sleep. When I'm at my worst my sleep pattern is all over the place. I very rarely have a problem falling to sleep. However I would quite often take my laptop to bed and watch a film until I felt tired which would be after 11pm. I slept well or so I thought and would wake up sometime between 11 and midday. This is really bad I know but it is what my body did but also when I woke up I would feel exhausted. I had no energy for the day and would just become Tracey "Jabba The Hut" Ward.

Following my system 'reboot' my sleep pattern improved considerably and these are my beliefs as to why this happened. I started by getting up the same time every day for 4 weeks. Every day I got into a routine of waking up at 7.30am, shower, breakfast (shake or smoothie) and walk the dog.

Now I will be honest with you this was a complete shock to my body, emotionally and physically. I hated it. I absolutely detested it and my body was telling me to go back to bed but I had to push myself; failure was completely out of the question. Needless to say by the end of the first weekend I was physically exhausted.

However, I stuck at it; I seriously thought I couldn't cope with it though. I would set my alarm at 7.30 every morning forcing myself not to hit snooze. I didn't like waking up at this time because it wasn't something my body could cope with but I kept on doing it. Eventually I found that I was waking up naturally at 8am without setting my alarm. Not only was I waking up at this time I actually felt awake. My head was clearer, my body for the first time in absolutely ages felt like it had slept. Even days when I said to myself that I could have a lay in as it was the weekend I was still waking up at 9 at the latest and rather than get a coffee or stay in bed for longer I would be up and ready to go downstairs. So however horrible it makes you feel at the start just keep doing it and it will start to get easier I promise.

I had a chat with a nutritionist and we talked about my eating habits. I would watch films on the laptop in my bed. This was a fantastic opportunity for me to stuff my face with sherbet lemons, chocolate, biscuits, crisps you name it. The nutritionist suggested to me that I need to stop watching films in bed. Just use the bed for sleep. Maybe read a few pages of a book but no more and this is the routine I implemented alongside the bedtime routine. It did feel wrong to start with but I'm in a routine now and it is a far better one.

If you find the above does not help then try the following 5 tips:

1. **Stick to the same bedtime every evening.** In the long run, this will help your body prepare for sleep at that time.
2. **No coffee after 2 pm** unless it is de-caf.
3. **Limit your alcohol intake to three hours before bedtime.** While booze might make you woozy, it worsens the quality of your sleep.
4. **Limit exercise in the four hours before bedtime.** Physical activity can make you feel wound up and make it difficult to go to sleep for several hours afterwards.
5. **Get 15 minutes of sunlight every day.** This is good for your circadian rhythm (your "body clock").

Finally, make sure that your bedroom is dark enough and stays at a pleasant temperature. Sleep well!

Sleep Improvement Summary

What I suggest you do is for at least one month preferably two is to set your alarm clock in the morning for the same time every day.

Do not under any circumstances hit snooze. Put your alarm clock or watch somewhere in your room so that you actually have to physically get out of bed to turn it off.

Get up and have a drink of cold water

At night do not use your phone or laptop in bed. Research has recently shown that the light given off by these devices is not actually good for making you feel sleepy. If you have to use these get yourself some amber glasses which change the blue light.

Read a book. I used to always read before I went to bed and haven't done for years. This is a habit I have now got back into and so glad I have. It enables me to switch off and before I know it I'm half asleep.

If you don't read download an audible book and listen to it with the lights off. There are so many amazing books to download.

Remember do this religiously for at least four weeks and if possible try and do it for eight you will then find your sleep pattern has been reset and you will be feeling more energetic during the day.

Drink More Water

Keeping your body hydrated is so extremely important. Not drinking enough water was something that I have been guilty of for a very long time. I have now been drinking between 2 - 3 litres of water a day, it took me a few weeks to get there and you will go to the toilet a lot at the beginning but hang on in there. It is important though that you spread this water throughout the day and do not drink it all in one go as that can be dangerous. Experts say do not drink more than 800ml of water an hour.

A good way to test if you are drinking enough water is to look at the colour of your urine. The clearer it is the better and obviously the darker it is means you need to drink more. Pretty obvious right. It is amazing how many people don't really check the colour of their urine after going or do but don't do anything about it. Listen to your body and drink more water.

If you are like me then you can add things to it to make it taste better. Infuse it with mint, lemon, an orange slice or a lime slice, cucumber, all sort of things.

Confession time - yep I did used to drink too much coffee. I have now switched to decaffeinated black tea and only drink up to 3 in the morning then after midday stick to water and I don't allow myself to have a tea until I have drank a whole beaker/bottle of water. I am now drinking plenty and my urine is looking good; too much information maybe but thought I would share that little pearl with you.

Now as I have just said I use the "must drink a bottle before I can have a tea" for you it might be something as simple as setting a timer on your phone. Whatever it is you need to do just do it.

Just remember that drinking enough water is absolutely critical. You need plenty of water not only for hydration, but proper bowel, kidney and liver function and also it will help with the suppression of hunger. Water suppresses the appetite naturally and some say it actually helps your body to speed up its own metabolism which in effect helps you to burn fat.

People who do not drink enough could be well on the way to producing kidney stones which can be extremely painful. What a lot of people don't realise is that if your kidneys are not getting enough water to work properly then the liver will step in to help. However, one of the livers main jobs is to metabolise your stored fat into energy, but it can not do this if it is helping out your kidneys. Subsequently the fat stores will stay in your body.

Drinking the right amount of water also helps the body to digest the food that you eat, it helps to prevent constipation. Believe it or not it also helps you feel more awake and even energetic. I know this for a fact! Also remember to increase your water levels on hot days and days that you exercise.

I must admit when I started this process I drank my water in a beautiful glass, added ice and a slice of lemon or lime or sometimes both and it helped me no end at the beginning. You can also add fresh ginger, strawberries and cucumber - get creative and see what you like. I would also put them in my water beaker along with sprigs of mint, basil just about anything to make it look more appetising. I now don't need to do that but at the weekends if I have sparkling water I still use the ice and slice method.

Drink More Water Summary

Drink a glass of water on waking and preferably cold.

Set a timer on your phone to remind you.

Add fruit and vegetable for infusions

Check the colour of your urine if it's dark you are not drinking enough.

Women drink a minimum of 2 litres a day.

Men drink a minimum of 2.5 litres a day

Exercise - Move that Body

This goes without question we all know that to lose weight and stay healthy we need to move our bodies. We need to become more active and incorporate exercise into our daily lives. I don't just mean heading off to the gym and pound the treadmill for two hours. I mean incorporate moving into your life in a natural way also.

Get off the bus a stop early, walk to the local shop instead of driving, run up the stairs instead of walk, do some squats while waiting for the kettle to boil, walk the dog before breakfast, do some bicep curls or tricep dips while the adverts are on. The list is endless and once you make it part of your natural day it will just become second nature.

Walking is one of the best exercises you can do and it is free. This is something that I really struggled with. Due to the fibromyalgia and a dodgy hip I'm not good at long distance walking due to the pain and also not being able to get back if the pain is too bad. My way around this is to go to the gym as I can walk on the treadmill until my body is telling me to stop and that way I don't have to worry about being stranded somewhere. It has turned it into a far better experience and walking as exercise doesn't scare me anymore.

Another thing about walking why not go somewhere nice to do it. Find a local beauty spot next to a river, through a forest, there must be lots of places local to you where you can go and just breathe in the fresh air, and seriously look around you at your surroundings while you do it, notice the flowers, the birds, nature in general. For a lot of people it's like a meditation and it can clear your head and at the same time you're having a good gentle workout.

As well as aerobic activity as described above it is important to do some resistance exercises. You can do these using your bodyweight or with free weights i.e dumbbells, kettlebells etc. Don't push yourself too hard start slowly, learn the moves and techniques accurately and then build up the weights. I can't do push ups and if you can't too try standing facing a wall and place your hands out in front of you and push off from the wall. There are always alternatives to exercises for people less able; even chair exercises. There are a lot of great apps too that you can download which can help you with this.

If you go to the gym make an appointment and learn some new exercises and get your technique checked as you don't want to cause any injuries. But for people like me reaching that "age" come on guys we are not getting younger strength exercises are even more important especially for women and the prevention of osteoporosis. Building muscle also increases your metabolism and you burn fat while not exercising.

Also it doesn't have to be boring find an exercise that you actually like, circuits, horse riding, running, golf, swimming, fencing (no not the garden variety) the list again is endless. Also mix it up don't do the same thing every time. Not only does your body get used to it but it can then become boring and you will give up and we don't want that to happen do we.

But think about what you are going to do and plan it realistically. It is very important to not go from not doing any exercise to running like Usain Bolt in one go. It is important to listen to your body as it will certainly tell you when it is tired. Start off gently by walking, yoga, swimming and gradually increase it the fitter and more energetic you get. A lot of people feel too embarrassed to go the gym because of their size. There is no need for this at all. When I go to the gym now I admire these guys tremendously because I was there once and it lifts my spirits to see them reaching for their goals. I just want to go up to them and give them a high five. I am definitely no gym bunny but I don't feel like the outsider I thought I would.

I used to get a sweat on even when people mentioned the word exercise. It was certainly some kind of horrible torture you put yourself through but I can honestly say now it is something I find most of the time enjoyable. I go with my daughter and we both come out relieved it is over but also smiling. We walk more upright and with purpose. What is not to like about that. It also keeps you motivated to not ruin all your hard work by eating rubbish.

Exercise Summary

If you have a dog then walk it at least twice a day. Do the first walk before your breakfast; believe me you will finish the walk quicker. In fact if you don't have a dog why not get a dog and while you are at it try the rescue centres you are killing two birds with one stone there or volunteer to walk someone else's. Remember a dog is for life though and only get one if you can dedicate the right amount of time to it.

Incorporate exercise into your every day routines

Find something you enjoy doing

When the weather is nice get yourself out and fill your lungs with fresh air and get that all important Vitamin D. Do some arm exercises while the adverts are on.

Squats or calf raises while the kettle is boiling.

Start gentle and work your way up.

Relax - Time Out

It is so important for you to be able to switch off every day for at the very least 15 minutes. Everyone is rushing about far too much these days and juggling so many things at the same time and then they worry why they get ill or are heading for a heart attack. Just slow down... right now and...... breathe!

We do it naturally, we don't need to tell our bodies to breathe. But a lot of us don't notice our breathing most of the time. When you get five minutes just stop and do what is called 3 - 4 - 5 breathing. This is so so easy and I've taught my daughter to do it now as she gets far too stressed. Drop your shoulders open up your chest and take a deep breath in from your nose for 3 seconds... now hold it for 4 seconds and then breathe it out through your mouth for 5. Give it a go right now... go on humour me... breathe in 1, 2, 3 and hold 1, 2, 3, 4 breathe out gently for 1, 2, 3, 4, 5. How easy was that? Keep doing it for a couple of minutes and you should feel yourself getting calmer with each breath.

Meditation is also a great tool to learn. Again it is not difficult it is just a case of sitting comfortably, and focus on your breath try not to think about anything but the breath. Images and words will come and go but just acknowledge them and let them drift on. There are some amazing apps available to help you with meditation "Headspace" is one of them and "Calm". I also have some guided meditations on my blog site www.traceyward.me that you can download. You will notice a huge difference in yourself once you get used to it. Also it might be worth looking up mindfulness apps too. I think as a society we are becoming increasingly aware of these things but quite often people are scared of the unknown or think you have to be a buddhist to mediate which is a load of rubbish. It is all about you and finding your inner space and that sense of calmness in this crazy world.

Yoga is a fantastic way to relax too. If you don't want to go to a class again you can find great tutorials online.

Play - playing is so important. We turn into adults and lose that inner child well most of us do I know I almost did. Get yourself a new hobby and give yourself some time out. I like painting and also if I don't have time to paint I use an adult colouring book and some gorgeous felt tip pens. I used to love paint by numbers as a kid. Believe you me my heart rate drops when I do this kind of thing.

Think back to when you were a child and a teenager what did you do that you really enjoyed? Then do that. It doesn't matter what age you are, it doesn't matter if you think you can't paint if you have always wanted a go then do it. It's not as difficult as you think and ultimately no one needs to see it but you anyway; just enjoy and get lost in the process of it all.

Time Out Summary

3-4-5 breathing when stressed.

Learn to meditate and take 10 minutes out a day

Try something like Yoga, Tai Chi etc

Celebrate your inner child. Take up new hobbies and rediscover old ones.

Love Yourself

Seriously guys we need to learn to do this. I spent my whole life near enough not liking myself. I put myself down in every way possible and at every given opportunity. Telling myself I was a rubbish mother, a rubbish partner, deserved all the bad things that kept happening. It took me 50 years to realise what a load of bollocks this was. It is amazing how we forget the good things that we have done and who we really are and what we have achieved in life to this point.

To readdress this I started listing my accomplishments over the years and I'll share some of them with you now so you can see what I mean and where I am going with this.

I am a fantastic mother - I have raised three amazing children more or less on my own and quite often under stressful circumstances. They now have their own lives, my eldest is doing something that he loves, my middle son has just finished University and my youngest has also started up her own little business. I have the most adorable grandsons and am looking forward so much to having others. All three of my children are in fantastic relationships and are happy. What more can I ask for as a mother?

I have a great sense of humour. This is definitely an asset a smile and a good giggle goes a long way in my eyes. I am also a "Laughing Yoga Practitioner". The power of laughter is so underrated. My daughter and I at home have some of the most belly aching laughs about things. It's just the best feeling.

I moved from Leicester to Harrogate after my marriage ended. That takes balls. I left everything and everyone I loved to make a fresh start. I missed my home for a long time (and worried about taking my eldest son further from his Dad) I still do but moving here was the right thing to do so I am now at peace with that decision.

I am a survivor of domestic violence which my children witnessed far too many times to mention. This happened in more than one relationship. I felt like I was a knob head magnet but I have changed my mindset. I am not a victim I am a survivor and have learnt so much about myself, my wants and my needs and appreciate the small things in life and things that others take for granted. I am blessed and at peace.

I am still single but I am happy. You don't need someone else to make you happy you can do that yourself.

Before this realisation I was far too needy. Yes I am happier in a loving relationship but until that happens I am now happy in my own skin, my own company and about the things I have on the horizon.

Following a very painfully sad relationship break up I felt ugly and fat and decided to take burlesque lessons to boost my self esteem and confidence. It worked! I loved every second of it and since that time I have been going from strength to strength.

I graduated from University with a First Class BA(Hons) in Art & Design and this was while becoming homeless due to domestic violence and having a babe in arms, a toddler and my eldest at primary school. But.. I did it! I was then rehoused and I dealt with being a single parent.

I've gone from not being able to walk up the stairs to running up them and I've done that in 3 months. My health has been appalling since about 1998 and gradually got worse over these years subsequently ending with a diagnosis of Fibromyalgia. Which I have just started to tackle head on and feeling the benefits of it now.

I set up an online support group for people suffering with depression, anxiety, PTSD and other mental health issues. This group has been going for the past five years now and it is an amazing bunch of people. I hope this year to find a meeting place somewhere for us all to meet up and have a coffee. I am constantly trying to raise awareness of mental health.

There are a lot of other things I could write about but I think that is enough to give you a better picture. I bet if you start writing about your accomplishments you will start to remember other things that you have done.

Also how you see yourself can be very different to how others see you. You might be pleasantly surprised. My self confidence was terrible but people I knew only had nice things to say about me but I would always think they were just saying it. But guess what?.. **yes I am a nice person**.

I have spent my life worrying about what other people thought of me. What a waste of precious time that is. It's none of your business what others think about you the only person you should be thinking about is yourself.

I don't mean in a selfish way you should always be there to help others but you need to start doing things that make you happy too. That is where I went wrong. Too busy letting other people get their own way in life and just follow in the background like a little sheep; too worried to step out of line. Well I'm telling you now is the time for you to step out of line. If you want to do something thats a bit crazy do it!. Dye your hair pink, pierce your nose, wear bright colours, anything that you want to do if it doesn't hurt anyone else do it. Life is too short and I don't know about you but I don't want to have any regrets.

I'm nearly 52 and I am not going to waste anymore of my life trying to make others happy without including myself in the process. I will always naturally try to because that is in my nature and it makes me feel good in myself but I will definitely start doing more for myself now. Grab life by the balls and ride it!

Love Yourself Summary

List your accomplishments from as far back as you can remember however little you think they are.

Write a list of words that describe you and then ask a friend to do the same too.

Put yourself first more.

Live out your dreams

Pamper Yourself With Non-Food Rewards

As well as time out as written above you do need to pamper yourself and find something you can indulge yourself in. Go on - book yourself a treatment at a beauticians. Why not book yourself a manicure or pedicure every time you lose 7lbs. Every month book yourself a full body massage. Quite often we are charging around doing 100 things at the same time and end up feeling and looking a bit worse for wear. I know these procedures are not cheap but you can get them done at local beauty colleges for a fraction of the price and this is what I do.

My advice is to take one day a week to have a soak in the bath. Get yourself some of your favourite bubble bath, bath bombs or buy a special candle, and relax and listen to your favourite music. Give yourself a manicure or pedicure. Get yourself a special fluffy towel a big one. Cover yourself in a gorgeous smelling body lotion. Give your skin some TLC and put on your fresh pj's and a squirt of your favourite perfume to just make you feel good. Put your feet up watch a film, or read a magazine. Just give yourself a day off sometimes because you deserve it. Actually schedule it into your diary or calendar. You will feel better for it I promise. I can't stress enough how important this is to make yourself feel good and special.

Pamper Yourself Summary

Treat yourself to some new beauty products so you feel as if you are indulging yourself that goes to men too as there are some fabulous mens products about these days. Liz Earle is my favourite and also Boots No 7 do a good selection.

Don't feel guilty about taking time out to do this you need to feel pampered and nourished and indulgent.

Light some beautiful smelling candles. Jo Malone and The White Company do some amazing candles but they are not cheap. When people ask you what you want for Christmas or Birthdays put one on your list. Also you can get some really nice candles from T K Maxx. I do make my own and might actually start selling them in the future.

Buy yourself some new clothes.

Laugh - Lots

I've known for a long time the importance of laughter but when I was filmed for the ITV documentary, The Fast Fix, it really struck me how much it is needed in your life. Remember I was feeling vulnerable anyway, I was overweight, my health and fitness levels were appalling and honestly I was lonely. So I was thrown into the lion's den so to speak. As a child and a young adult I was painfully shy and wouldn't have coped with this situation at all back then but I seem to have lost a lot of my shyness over the past few years. I can be quiet but that's just me but here I was meeting four other people and I am going to let them see me at my worst and be filmed doing it.

I was very fortunate because I felt I got on with everyone in the house and also the crew. You have your favourites it is only natural but I had a deep love and affection for Steve and Luke, two of my housemates. I would have struggled without these two we just clicked straightaway. Those two guys just got me 100%, they knew when I was upset and would just come up and give me a hug and it was that way for the three of us all the way through the process. The three amigos, the three musketeers you get the picture.

I am talking about these two because we all bounced off each other. I can say hand on heart I have never laughed so much in my life as I did in that house. That laughter was like cement holding the bricks together. I'm talking serious laughing here, belly laughs, crying with laughter. Laughing until you ache is just the best feeling. But I found that it stays with you for a long time. It certainly got me through and I know it did too with Steve and Luke. In fact to this day if I close my eyes I can still hear those two taking the piss out of each other and can still hear their amazing laughs.

Have a think to yourself and try and remember when you had the last really good belly laugh? I am so lucky that I have so many belly laughs with my children. It is something magical it lifts you so much. As I recently mentioned I am now doing laughter yoga; and because of lockdown I will be taking it online along with guided mediations and coaching for people. There is no yoga as such it is about playing and laughing and it has proven positive effects on you physically and emotionally.

The thing with laughing too it is infectious. One time during the documentary we had to travel to Newcastle by train and on the way back I was sat next to Steve. I can't even remember what it was we were laughing about now but something started us off. The laughing just got louder and louder and more and more out of control but the amazing thing was the people around us were joining in and they didn't know what the joke was.

It was wonderful to see and experience but when they started laughing that set me and Steve off again. But after you have a laughing session like that you feel 10lb lighter you feel really lifted.

Quite often at night while in bed I listen to some podcasts; my favourite is Ricky Gervais, Steve Merchant and Karl

Pilkington. I seriously laugh out loud so many times; isn't that an amazing way to fall asleep? Giggling and with a smile on your face.

Laughing Summary

Don't take life too seriously; try and find the humour in everyday situations.
Try and do more fun things with friends and family.

Get yourself a little five year diary. If something really funny happened one day write about it. You will be amazed at when you look back and read it you will remember it and smile. In fact write anything positive that happened; at least one thing per day. When you have a day and you are not feeling that good have a quick flick through and you will be smiling by the end of it both inside and outside.

Get Out Of Your Comfort Zone

I can not express enough how important this is. I only learnt this lesson when I was 47 but wish I it had happened a lot earlier. So hopefully you will read this and take it on board what I am about to say.

I'll give you a bit of background so you can see where I am coming from. Over the years I knew I wanted to be self-employed and kept coming up with great ideas but got nowhere. Why was that? it wasn't because they were rubbish ideas it was because I couldn't face pushing myself forward. I was scared of failure. I was scared of looking stupid, I was scared of attention negative and positive. I was a bit of an introvert. I didn't like not being out of my comfort zone which was selling myself and actually believing in myself. Well if I don't believe in myself no one else will right?

So simple really and such an important thing. You need to start believing in yourself. You need to put yourself out there. Own that attitude and believe. The power is within; I had it tattooed on my inner arm as a constant reminder! No you don't need to get a tattoo.

What I am trying to say is you will get nowhere on this planet without pushing yourself forward and keep doing that. Think of yourself maybe as standing on the bottom rung of that ladder. You know you want to get to the top of it but you can only start doing that by taking another step, and another and another until you get there. So how do you this? You get yourself out of your comfort zone otherwise you just don't stand a chance. Each rung you take is getting you out of your comfort zone but it is getting you closer to where you want to be.

My problem is I'm rubbish or I was rubbish at this so I knew I had to do it if I wanted to succeed with anything. I had been doing my online support group, published my own poetry book and had decided I wanted to get a collection of poems from people suffering with mental health issues to raise awareness. I knew this wasn't going to come to fruition if I didn't sell myself. The easy thing was I believed in what I was doing 100% so I had the passion there; I just had to show the world that. And you are now reading it.

That bit is out of my comfort zone the selling myself bit but if I didn't sell myself this book would get nowhere. So I decided to write to the local newspaper and tell them what I was doing and asked if they were interested.

I'll be honest when I clicked on "send" I felt sick to the stomach. I thought they are just going to laugh, say thanks but no thanks and all those kinds of things. But what happened? They wrote back straightaway. By the end of that day I was on the phone talking to a reporter and arranging a photoshoot to go with the article in the paper. I was completely and utterly gobsmacked and this started things in motion.

The old Tracey would have just not sent the email. The new Tracey sent it and started a snowball effect. I am now as I write this in the UK's bestselling writing magazine with an article about the same thing and am receiving poetry from all over the world for this project.
I now have to find a publisher to get this book out there. This is where the old Tracey would be cowering behind the curtains stressing about getting rejected. The new Tracey is now determined and on a mission and will be for the rest of my life.

Get Out Of Your Comfort Zone Summary

You have to push yourself.

You need to recognise that scary feeling you get in the pit of your stomach is not a not a bad thing it is a good thing. That feeling is actually a really good feeling because it means that you are taking that next step on that ladder. You are moving up and it is scary but remind yourself it is also exciting.

Be a rebel, throw caution to the wind and take that next step, make that phone call, write that email. What is the worst that can happen? Nothing! Nothing is what will happen. So what are you waiting for? Do it and do it now! Stop being reactive and be proactive.

Read and Continue to Learn New Things

Stop being complacent and stop being in a rut that's a really boring place to be. Learn new things and I don't mean once a year do it all your life. There is so much we don't know or understand. I love learning new things not only does it give you new things to talk about but it gives you a greater understanding of you and the world you live in. Surely that is a good thing right?

Read more whether it is just for pleasure such as a novel or self help books, health books, science books, history books, nature books there must be a subject out there you are interested in so why don't you get yourself a book. There is also a library you can use so use them. It's free and some of the libraries out there are just incredible. The one in Harrogate I absolutely love; it is a beautiful old building and so big inside with different areas to do different things. A coffee machine, wifi access, reading areas I just love it.

Reading gives a lot of people so much pleasure. It is another way to escape the day to day monotony; it is a little bit of escapism, somewhere you can just disappear to and forget all the crap going on in the world.

Book yourself on a course. There are so many courses ran at schools in the evenings. It is also a good way to make new friends.

Read and Learn New Things Summary

Find out where your local library is and pay it a visit.

Look for a local book club
Take a trip to your local bookshop and have a good walk around I am certain you will find something that peaks your interest.

If you don't want to buy loads of books get yourself a Kindle. These little guys are tremendous. You can take them anyway and they fit in your bag so easily.

Look at the courses that are running local to you.

Make A Difference

I have this service to humanity thing running through my veins and I always have done. I'm quite a spiritual person and get a tremendous amount of pleasure and contentment in caring for other people, making people smile and making a difference to someones day. It gives me an inner peace and lightness.

I write about this in my blog quite often. I truly believe we are spiritual beings living in physical bodies. The reason we are here is Love, Compassion, and Empathy. These three things make up my spiritual body and to nourish those and keep them topped up I have to make a difference; it's that simple.

I try and do something every single day even if it is just to smile at a complete stranger. Open the door for someone, listen to someone, help someone with something, give a random stranger some flowers, do something for charity, let a car driver out, become a visitor in a nursing home (you'd be amazed by how many residents never get visitors).

I'm in the process of getting involved with the disabled riders group and also a mental health awareness campaign. Some things you do; part of the process is shouting about it but the other things just keep to yourself.

The pleasure and wonderful feeling it creates is yours and it belongs inside you but at the same time giving you a lovely connection with the other person. It is amazing the difference one simple act of kindness can make on someones day and life. We get so caught up in our own little bubble we stop looking out for others. We need to converse with our fellow man. Talk to strangers you never know you might find the love of your life or a friend for life.

I have been going to the gym and I watch all the people coming and going. Doing their exercise most of the time with headphones on which is fine I do the same. However some of the things I do at the gym I have to take them out and then it strikes me how we keep ourselves to ourselves. To me that makes it seem more of a chore rather than something enjoyable. This week I was in the gym's separate kinesis room. There was me and two other ladies in it; I recognised them I have seen them in there countless times but we never acknowledge each other. I was doing some tricep exercises and got to the end of the last set and was seriously feeling it. I just turned to the lady next to me laughed and said something along the lines of, "God the things we put ourselves through" and she laughed and then the other lady said something. The atmosphere instantly lifted and we carried on with a smile on our faces and when each lady left they said a few words and goodbye which I thought was great.

It's funny as a child I was painfully shy; I mean seriously shy. I struggled to find my voice, I would get anxious in situations where I would have to talk to someone. I think life has given me a pair of bollocks the size of an elephant and I'm so grateful for them. If you want big bollocks too then do as I do and make a difference not only to others but to yourself. Stay true to yourself and your beliefs.

I promise you that making a difference to someone else's life improves your own. Don't expect anything back in return because you won't get anything physical maybe a smile or a hug but those things and the way it will make you feel will be priceless.

I call it the ripple effect. Nine times out of ten if you let a car out at a junction they will do so also and it goes on like that creating a wave of good deeds. You don't know what other people have going on in their lives. They could be having an absolute day of hell. I feel extremely lucky to be where I am. I don't have a lot to my name but I have my health, the love of a beautiful family, the overwhelming love of grandchildren, food on my table and clothes on my back. There are a lot of people out there a lot worse than me.

I truly believe that the richer you make other peoples lives the richer you become in so many other ways. I don't care if people think I'm a fruit loop that's their opinion and they are entitled to it but it is my belief and I'm sticking with it.

I aim to be a role model not only to my children and grandchildren but to everyone I meet. There is no way around it you will always leave an impression with everyone that you meet in life. What that impression is will be up to you. The ball is in your court.. What impression would you like them to go away with?

Nourish Your Body With The Right Food

In my "old" life every day was a treat day but it just made me sick and it made me ill. I didn't even feel good after eating the stuff. I was slowly killing myself.

Food should be enjoyable but at the same time you need to remember it is also fuel for your body. A good thing to do is learn about the human body, what and where the muscles are, how they work, learn about the central nervous system. Also learn what happens to your body when you eat rubbish, when you eat healthy, what happens when you exercise. The human body is an amazing bit of kit so get to know it and then you will know how to look after it. We take it all for granted and yes it works ok without us doing too much but how better would it work if you knew what actually made it work.

Nourish Your Body Summary

Eat the Rainbow

Eat single ingredient foods

Drink Plenty of water

Find a healthy balance of protein, carbohydrates and fats.

Avoid processed foods as much as possible. When you look at the ingredients list if you do not know what one of the ingredients looks like you probably should not be eating it.

Eat to live do not live to eat!

Try to stick to high fat, moderate protein and low carbs wherever possible.

While learning this use My Fitness Pal app as you can enter the foods you eat and it will show you where you are going wrong and help to re-educate you.

Reduce Your Stress Levels

Stress was a huge problem for me. I was constantly stressed. My body was in a constant state of flight or fight which is also called 'acute stress response". For those of you who do not know what this is I will try and explain.

The fight or flight response is your body's natural way of coping with a dangerous situation. Imagine that you live in a world that is full of predators and one day you are minding your own business walking along when all of a sudden a T-Rex jumps out in front of you. What would you do? How would you respond? If you didn't have this fight or flight response you would do nothing and get eaten there and then because your body wouldn't be able to react quickly enough and with enough strength to do anything about it. This is where your fight or flight response automatically kicks in.

That response is a flood of changes to your hormones, neurotransmitters and body to prepare it so you can immediately run away or stay and fight. Things like your blood flow will increase, it will keep your body cool, provide you with more energy helping you see and respond more quickly to Mr T Rex. So thanks to this fight or flight response you know when to feel fear and have the energy to run away and without hurting yourself in the process.

It is an important state that your body uses for example when driving, standing on a ledge of a building, walking down a dark alley etc. Your body automatically goes into the right mode to escape or fight. Your levels of alertness have automatically raised.

Where it goes wrong is when your fight or flight reaction switches itself on and there is no danger being present. Remember that the fight or flight response was not really designed for long term actions which is why it often causes muscle tension. This is not due to the direct actions of the fight or flight response, but the stress that the response puts on your body over the an extended period of time. There have been a few times in the past I have been prescribed Diazepam to help my body to relax because of this.

The fight or flight response also turns off or reduces some activity in certain parts of your brain, this is because in a dangerous situation these parts of your brain are less important and your mind only has a limited amount of resources and energy. When you have an anxiety disorder, your mind may continue to be affected by this, which creates issues like constipation, diarrhoea, bloating, and even nerve dysfunctions.

The good news is that in general none of these issues are dangerous, and if you can control your anxiety your entire body will be back to normal. Nothing is wrong with you when they occur, nor is any damage being done. The only problem is that anxiety is often self-sustaining, and there is some evidence that long term anxiety issues can actually weaken or damage your fight or flight response further.

Now if you follow everything I've suggested, then fingers crossed, your stress levels should reduce. So how do you address your mental health effectively if you don't like the sound of the above?

I'm sorry but it is that "E" word again. Yep you know the one; It starts with exercise, which should be priority number one. Exercise releases neurotransmitters that improve mood, burns away stress hormone and adrenaline, tires muscles to reduce anxiety symptoms and more. Exercise has been compared to some of the leading anti-anxiety medications and come out tied or ahead, all without a single chemical. If you're not exercising yet, you should be at whatever pace that may be best for you.

Healthy living in general can play a role too. While anxiety doesn't usually develop because of the foods you eat or your lifestyle choices, studies have shown that anxiety coping is better when you get a full night's sleep, drink enough water, and try your best to cut down on stress producing activities.

Chronic stress may increase levels of stress hormones such as cortisol in your body. This can cause increased hunger and result in weight gain and obviously on the slippery path to becoming a type 2 diabetic which we are really trying to avoid.

If you're looking to lose weight, you should review possible ways to decrease or better handle excessive stress in your life. Although this often demands substantial changes, even altering small things – such as posture – may immediately affect your stress hormone levels, and perhaps your weight. It sounds daft but consciously trying to keep your shoulders down actually helps during stressful situations. I learnt this from a midwife while giving birth and it is so very true.

Diet hasn't been shown to play a strong role in anxiety, but since a healthier diet can help you feel better in general, it may be of benefit too. What do you have to lose just give it a go.

To Summerise:

Get enough sleep

Drink More Water

Exercise - move that body

Relax and take time out

Breathe In Fresh Air and get some Vitamin D from the sun.

Love Yourself and rediscover who you are

Pamper Yourself With non-food rewards

Laugh - lots

Get out of your comfort zone

Read and continue to learn new things

Make a difference

Nourish your body with the right foods

Reduce your stress levels and do all the above!

Finally I just want to remind you that you need to be realistic. These things can be changed and will be changed and I am living proof of this. But I think the best way to progress is by setting yourself small goals because you can not change overnight.

Remember this is a marathon and not a sprint.

But most importantly remember if you want to reach that winning line you will do; you just need to believe in yourself and want to. In the meantime, stay strong, stay focussed and take back control of your life.

You can do this!

A Darker Shade of Blue

Chapter 6

30 Things To Start Doing For Yourself

When I went into The Fast Clinic I'll admit I had lost my path somewhat and I was on a huge downward spiral. I'd never been so ill, so low and so fed up and angry with myself. I'd got myself into such a state and my health was just getting worse by the day. If my daughter wasn't at home I would have just become a recluse. The Fast Fix gave my mental and physical health a re-set and a huge one. So let's see if I can help you with that too.

I want you to look at each one of these and read them; I don't want you to rush through the list. The only exception is that you read through the list quickly but then go back to the start and digest each one and really think about it until you think you can fully relate to it. So here we go:

Spend Time With The Right People

Speaks for itself really doesn't it. We all have those people in our lives or have had them in our lives that just drain you physically and emotionally. If they aren't giving anything positive into your life you don't need them. They are like emotional leeches sucking the life right out of you. Get rid!

Facing Your Problems Head On

It is no good putting something in the back of your mind that you know you need to deal with. Firstly it causes you undue stress and stress that can be dealt with. The thought of doing something you don't want to is actually worse than doing it. Having it hanging there in the background all the time I've been there so many times and thought to myself afterwards what the hell was I worried about.

If you actually stop for a minute take a few breaths then take control of the situation you will actually feel empowered. You will feel empowered and relieved when you realise you it wasn't anywhere near as bad as you thought it would be. So what you were worrying for? Just do it!

Being Honest With Yourself

This is so important if you can't be honest with yourself you are living a false life. Are you pretending to be someone you are not just to try and impress someone you don't know? It's ridiculous because the real you will come out eventually then what will happen is heartache and sadness. If you believe in yourself and what you stand for you will feel so much better and people will feel much better around you. You can't live a lie.

Make Your Own Happiness A Priority

This is something I should have done years ago. I have spent my life constantly making other people happy instead of myself. It is absolutely ridiculous. You can be in a relationship that you know isn't working but you carry on with it because you don't want to hurt them. But you are happy to hurt yourself by being in a broken relationship, suffering, miserable – just why? Why do we do that? You need to make yourself happy then make others happy.

Sometimes you need to be selfish and this is being selfish in a good way. Your own happiness is vital to be healthy emotionally and physically. As I have said before you can not pour from an empty cup.

Being Yourself Genuinely And Proudly

This goes alongside being honest with yourself. You need to be yourself. If you want to shave all your hair off shave it off. A bit extreme but you know what I mean. As long as being a genuine version of yourself does not hurt anyone else then do it and be proud. Don't live your life with regrets. It was the same with me I desperately wanted pink hair and I was wrestling with the decision thinking about what other people would say etc. I did it though and loved it at the time I did it which wasn't for long but I'm still glad I did it.

Noticing And Living In The Present

We all do this, worry about what happened yesterday and worry about what is going to happen tomorrow. So just think for a minute what happened yesterday you can't change it, not at all, it is done end off so stop sweating the small stuff. Same goes with tomorrow because tomorrow does not exist what exists is you right now, this very second. Live in that moment and make the most of it.

My Mother lives in the past. She is still caught up in the moment my Father left her for someone else. Yes, it was a horrible experience but holding on to things like that is not going to do you any good. If it is something bad that happened in the past you need to be able to accept it, forgive and then move on. Because if you don't it can be it will cause physical illness and emotional illness. You have to remember that life is about having lessons, we learn form these things and it makes us a better person but if you let it.

Valuing The Lessons Your Mistakes Teach You

This relates to the previous one. If you don't learn from your mistakes you will keep doing them again and again until you do. Each mistake you make is something very valuable. When you realise you are beating yourself up about something just stop and think. Think about the mistake, why you made it, what could you have done differently, and how are you going to move on from it.

Being More Polite To Yourself

A lot of us are quite rude and horrible to ourselves. Putting ourselves down in front of other people as a way of coping with something but it's so wrong.

When I was at my largest I would constantly put myself down and turn my size into a joke but inside it wasn't funny in the slightest. I'd laugh with everyone else but inside I was in turmoil and embarrassed and my self-esteem was non-existent. You need to start being kind to yourself. The kinder you are to yourself the happier you will be and it will have a knock on effect on the people around you.

Enjoying The Things You Already Have

A lot of us sit and think I've got nothing, so and so has an amazing sofa I wish I had one, so and so has the best car and mine is a piece of junk. The list goes on and on. But if you sat down and looked around yourself at what you actually have you are really quite blessed.

The majority of people have more things than they need. So take yourself through each room if you need to and just take in what you actually have. It will be more than enough to live your life and be happy. Things are just that "things". So what if you don't have the latest Porsche as long as the car you have takes you from A to B then on the scale of things it really doesn't matter.

Giving Your Ideas And Dreams A Chance

Now I am living proof of this. The first thing you need to do is sit down with a pen and a bit of paper (or my book: ***Rediscover Who You Really Are and Where You Want To Be Using My List of 111 Questions***) and list all of your dreams and ideas. The things you have wanted to do and to try. If you stay focused on your goal you will get there.

Ultimately it is up to you and not anyone else. These are your goals no one elses and it is up to you if you make them come true. These things don't just happen on their own you have to be pro-active here. It is fine saying I want to buy such and such a car then just leave it thinking it is just going to turn up on your doorstep because the chances are that just is not going to happen. So you need to sit and think about what you have to do to get to that final point and just do it!

Believing That You Are Ready For The Next Step

Belief in yourself and your own abilities is so important. If you don't believe in yourself you just won't move forward it is as simple as that. People tend to stay just where they are because they are scared of failure and comfortable with what the know. If you are scared of failure you will never win or move forward. By taking the next step you are getting closer to your goal and you won't get there without taking that step. We only move forward in life by putting ourselves out of our comfort zone.

This is a huge lesson that I learnt especially over the past couple of years. I am currently putting together an anthology, a selection of poems written by people suffering from different kinds of mental illness and this is to raise mental health awareness.

Now I am actually quite shy sometimes and used to have very little belief in my abilities. Now I knew that to get anywhere with this book that I would have to reach out for help because it wasn't going to write itself. What I did was send an email to the local newspaper asking if they could run a story about my proposed book and ask people to donate their own poems.

Before I clicked on "send" I was so nervous, I felt sick, I thought I wouldn't get a reply, I thought if I did get a reply it would be to say thanks but no thanks. I was putting myself out of my comfort zone here but I knew that I had to do it otherwise the book wouldn't happen. I clicked send. And guess what the sky didn't fall down, the house didn't collapse, what happened was I got a reply back that day from a reporter who believed in me and my project and wanted to run a story.

By the end of the week, I was at the newspaper office, getting my photo taken and my story was put in the newspaper the following week. What I want you to learn from this is that the feeling we get when we are out of our comfort zone is actually a very good feeling and not one to be scared of.

Because that is the feeling of taking the next step. Believe in yourself and take that step because it is a good thing; it is a good feeling.

Entering New Relationships For The Right Reasons

I am the world's expert on crap relationships. With the exception of my husband, I went from one bad relationship to another. I was caught up in this vicious circle that I just couldn't seem to get out of.

Now I think I'm quite intelligent but when it came to men I was making serious mistakes. This is because I didn't have self-respect, I had low self-esteem, I felt guilty for the breakdown of my marriage and my son not having his father by his side, I was in effect punishing myself the whole time. Convinced I wasn't worthy of a good man I would settle for second best because that is all I thought deserved.

What I have come to learn is that I don't need a man to make me happy I've actually made myself happy and that is so very important. Because now when a man comes along I will be with him for all the right reasons. I'm happy being me and I'm no longer needy.

If someone doesn't show me the love and respect I deserve then it is just not going to happen. I would rather be single than be with someone who puts me down, etc. Do you know what? They should be happy and privileged to have me. That is one thing I have never said to myself before.

You see I know now that I am actually ok, I'm alright, I deserve better than I've had.

I want a relationship now and someone I can spend the rest of my life with. To enrich my life and to bring good things into it by sharing it with someone else and vice versa.

Giving New People You Meet A Chance

Not everyone is comfortable when you meet someone new. And although I know that first impressions count you do need to remember that for a short time that person could just be really nervous, or have low self-esteem etc.

It can actually take a few meetings before someone comes out of their shell. Take me, for example, I can be quite shy with people I don't know. But the people that really know me have seen the other side and I can actually be very funny when I am comfortable with someone. As people we are multi-faceted; we have so many sides we really do. Different people bring out different qualities in you too. Be with people who can bring out the best side of you. Don't judge someone by looks alone; people can have some amazing qualities; beauty, after all, is only skin deep.

What is important is how someone makes you feel. Yes, you have to be attracted to someone but that can develop over a short space of time. Someone's personality is more important than their waist size.

Competing Against An Earlier Version Of Yourself

We are all guilty of this I think. In my head, I can still picture the 20-year-old version of myself, an amazing figure, long blonde hair, strutting her stuff in a white trouser suit and heels I was like a female John Travolta. I mean come on Wardy, those days are over.
I will never look like that again but then I don't need to either. What you need to be is today's version of yourself; whatever that may be. You can still look hot 30 years on; a lot of it is a "state of mind".

Marilyn Monroe could do this. She could walk down the street as Norma Jean and no one would notice but when she flicked that Marilyn Monroe switch everyone knew who she was. There is no need comparing yourself physically or emotionally to that person you were 20 years ago because that person is not you anymore.

You need to be confident in the you that lives right now. Compare yourself to no one. Flick that Marilyn Monroe switch right now and strut your stuff.

Cheering For Other People's Victories

This goes without saying. Whenever someone I know achieves something I am delighted for them and I make sure they know I am.

There are a lot of people out there who just get jealous of others and that is not an attractive quality. Why can't people just be happy for their friends and family? Ultimately, it comes down to their own insecurities and that is something you need to try and remember. It is nothing personal it is their problem to sort out not yours.

Everyone likes to be told well done, or get some praise for their efforts. And why shouldn't they because they've earned it?

Imagine you did something you were really proud of and no one acknowledges it, none of your friends or family. I find that quite sad. True friends and people with beautiful souls will cheer along their friends and be there for them to celebrate. Take a moment next time someone tells you something they are happy about and acknowledge them. It costs nothing and takes seconds.

Looking For The Silver Lining In Situations

Again this is about actively changing your mindset. I am a great believer in silver linings. You can always salvage something from a bad situation or act.

The worst case scenario is it's a life lesson we are meant to learn and it is how we move forward in life from that point. Always look for the positive. So many people just dwell constantly on the negative. They just wallow in a pool of self-pity getting nowhere fast. Some of them can't help it because that is how their brains are wired but what you need to do is be pro-active and not reactive.

Forgiving Yourself And Others

We have kind of touched on this slightly already but it deserves a point of its own because it is so important to be able to forgive not just yourself but others too. I have had a lot of bad experiences in my life but internally I have been able to forgive everyone who hurt me either deliberately or not and move on. And yes sometimes you don't forget. However, once you accept the situation and forgive either them or yourself or sometimes both you will be happy; genuinely happy.

Holding on to something or someone you can't forgive is just going to be more negativity and it will infect you like a disease turning you into someone bitter and angry and stressed. These are not good feelings to have and they have a negative impact on your emotional and physical health.

So think to yourself about people you need to forgive and find it in your heart to do so. Just as importantly forgive yourself for any mistake you have made. If you have truly learnt from your mistake then it is time to forgive yourself.

One thing I used to do years ago was to write on a piece of toilet roll someone's name in black. I would then flush it down the toilet and flush it away – easy!

Another way is to do a bit of visualisation. Imagine looking up at a beautiful blue sky and then you notice a little white fluffy cloud. Put that person into that cloud and find the more you think about it the blacker the cloud gets;

Fill it with all that negativity associated with that person and get that cloud all nice and black and then just visualise it just floating away until you can't see it anymore.

Helping Those Around You

This is something that is extremely important to me and is my sole mission in life and "soul" mission come to that. I am on a mission to make a difference in wherever way that I can and that is an important part of who I am. You should help those around you without expecting it in return. Helping others also sets off something I call a ripple effect. Chances are if you do a kind deed for someone they will go on to do the same for someone else.

These little things can mean such a lot to someone. You don't know what is happening in other peoples lives. Sometimes a simple smile or touch of a hand can have such a massive impact on someone's life. Be kind and be generous and be there to offer support. This is where empathy comes in because sometimes people are too scared to say they need help which brings me to the next point.

Listening To Your Own Inner Voice

Now I'm telling you here to trust your intuition as I'm telling you now your gut never lies to you. You just choose to ignore it because you don't want to face up to the truth of something or reality. I've been there myself and done it loads especially in abusive relationships. When that little alarm bell goes off; trust it and act on it. If you don't you will come to regret it.

Being Attentive To Your Stress Level And Take Short Breaks

Stress is a killer and the cause of so many problems. You need to learn to acknowledge it and deal with it. We all have different coping mechanisms but one of them is by taking a short break.

This could be anything from going for a walk, phoning a friend, going for a drive or sitting in the garden with a cuppa. If possible take short breaks also as in weekends away from the thing that stresses you and do something different and/or something that makes you smile and laugh.

Notice The Beauty Of Small Moments

We walk around a lot of the time with blinkers on we really do. I think I'm quite fortunate because as a creative person and an artist you tend to pick up on beauty in different ways. For me, I can sit and watch the wind through the trees and watch those leaves dancing about. Listening to and becoming aware of the birds singing around you. Noticing the joy in a child's face when they see something for the first time.

Someone's laughter, someone's smile, the effort someone has taken to do something small for you but realising the intention behind it was massive. If you think of it the day consists of a lot of beautiful small moments but we just don't see them because we simply don't look.

Accepting Things When They Are Less Than Perfect

How many of you beat yourself up when something isn't perfect. I'm not being funny here but perfection doesn't exist where you think it should. A lot of people strive to be perfect well that isn't going to work you just need to be the best version of yourself you can be. We all make mistakes and we are not perfect and that is what makes us unique. With regards to doing something badly, as long as you know you have done the best that you could then that is good enough. If you haven't then draw a line under it and carry on.

Working Towards Your Goal Every Day

This goes without question. Don't procrastinate you know what your goals are and you know what you have to do to get there so just do it. If you struggle with this kind of thing write a list. When you go to bed write a list of just 3 things that you need to accomplish the following day and do them.

I know some people like to write a huge list but sometimes this can be a bit overwhelming and when you don't tick them all off you start beating yourself up again. Three things are manageable and it will give you a sense of satisfaction for a job well done. Then go to bed and write another 3 things for the following day. Lists are underestimated they can really help you to achieve the things you want to. You could even start a journal and let it be something that you do every day.

Being More Open About How You Feel

Now we are not all psychic so we can't tell what is going on with other people. I have been guilty of keeping my sadness bottled up in the past and didn't talk to people about it. But I am seriously an open book. If someone asks me something they get an answer. I stay true to myself and to them and I personally don't think there is another way to be.

If I like someone they will know about it. I don't mess with peoples heads, and I don't expect others to mess with mine. This goes back to being true to yourself and others. The more open you are with people they more they will gravitate towards you and respond positively. It is also ok to show your vulnerable side we all have them pretending to be made of steel just doesn't work.

Taking Full Responsibility For Your Own Life

This is important you as you can't go through life blaming others for your misfortunes. This is your life, your life choices, your actions, your reasons for your actions, so if it goes tits up it is your doing and no one else's. It is all too easy to blame someone else for your overeating when really it is you that is putting it in your mouth. We blame

others because we don't want to admit we have failed or
done something wrong or are insecure.

If you act on all the previous points this bit will fall into
place. Accept your mistakes, forgive yourself for them and
then move on or change your circumstances otherwise, the
same crap will just keep happening.

Actively Nurturing Your Most Important Relationships

This is about not just your partner but your children, your
grandchildren, your friends, your parents, your pets;
everyone that you love or adds positivity and enhances
your life.   Don't ever take any of these people for granted
because life is too short and they deserve better from you.

It is amazing to love someone but show them you love
them they are not mind readers, do little things for them,
make them a cake, give them some flowers, send them a
card, go somewhere with them, phone them, make
something for them you know they will like.   The list is
seriously endless but show your affection and make them
feel loved and wanted and needed.

Concentrate On The Things That You Can Control

Now, first of all, only you can control what you put in your
mouth each and every day.   So concentrate on why you
need to **not** put certain things in your mouth.   Your body
needs loving and looking after and you are the only one

that can do that. It is the same for the rest of your life. What can you take control of? Your fitness levels for one. Your body needs to be able to move in order for you to do things you want to and need to. Think about all the things now that you can control and stick at it.

Focussing On The Possibility Of Positive Outcomes

You need the mindset of a top athlete. When they stand on the starting line what is going through their heads. Well, I will tell you what is going through their heads is the image of them at them being first at that finishing line. Nothing else at all. They are seeing it and feeling it and that is what you need to do.

If you think you have already achieved something in your head, and make it as real as you can in your mind's eye, i.e you have the mindset of a slim fit person, it will make that goal easier to attain.

Because you are now thinking as a slim healthy person. A slim healthy person won't want to eat the entire contents of a McDonald's menu. It is just not an option. Because you are now focusing on positive outcomes. Failure is just not an option.

Noticing How Wealthy You Are Right Now

And I am not just talking about money although you can include that if you wish. But what other areas in your life are you wealthy?

You have food, a bed, a home, a family, loved ones, the ability to be happy, healthy, creative, kind, caring. These are the things that are important. You could be extremely wealthy right now and you didn't even realise just how much.

I hope this has given you some things to think about and will help you to feel positive and uplifted about what lies ahead.

A Darker Shade of Blue

Other Books Written By Tracey Ward

It's Not Rocket Science - How To Reverse Type 2 Diabetes, Improve Your Life And Become A Better Version Of Yourself.

Following my time in the successful and groundbreaking ITV documentary The Fast Fix: Diabetes I wrote all about my time during this and also about my relationship with food both before and afterwards. It also addresses the emotional side of losing weight and gives you lots of things to do to help yourself on your journey.

It's Not Rocket Science: Diet Journal

A diet journal created to go alongside It's Not Rocket Science Reverse Type 2 Diabetes And Become A Better Version Of Yourself. It can also be used with any diet that you may be one. A daily journal to track what you have eaten, drank, exercise, mood followed by a 4 weekly measurements summary and a 3 monthly measurement summary. This diary will last you for 6 months. Included at the back some positive coping mechanisms and ways to move forward, focus and stay on goal.

Why Rainbows May Cry

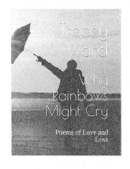

As my blog readers know I published my first book of poetry back in 2016. Why Rainbows May Cry was a hugely cathartic experience for me from the start to the end. I never intended to publish this as a book; the poetry was a way for me to express the emotions that I was experiencing and feeling at the time. The poems are about love and loss and the nightmare that is the world of online dating. I seemed to go from one disaster to another and the best way for me to deal with it was through poetry. This book will always mean a lot to me and the personal messages I have received from people that have read it has been overwhelming.

Rediscover Who You Really Are And Where You Want To Be - Using My List Of 111 Questions

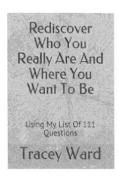

This book was initially created for a close friend who suffers from bi-polar, depression and anxiety and had lost his way in life. Unfortunately, when people struggle with mental health issues you can get bogged down and become extremely unfocused and basically can't see the wood for the trees. This happened to my friend.

I suggested that he wrote a list of things that made him feel happy etc but because of the place he was in emotionally, understandably he couldn't focus on thinking of any questions to ask himself for him to start this process. Subsequently, that gave birth to this book.

It's not an answer to all your problems because the answer is within you; all this book will do is make you think about different areas in your life. There is nothing too scary in there it is just a starting block to get you thinking of ways to start the process of moving forward and taking back control of your life. Moving forward in a way where you can be more pro-active rather than reactive.

This is so important I do this with myself all the time; I have a huge list of questions which I review on a very regular basis and I have found it a very positive thing to dip in and out of and hopefully, you will too. On another note I know there are people who just like writing lists and lists of lists; my lovely daughter-in-law and I are both guilty of this. Included at the back of the book is also space for a bucket list and also anxiety grounding exercises, and a list of ways to apply the important act of self-care. I hope it helps people going through a difficult time to re-focus their thoughts even for a short time.

All books are available to buy on Amazon.

A Darker Shade of Blue

NOTES

HelpGuide: Authors: Melinda Smith, M.A., Lawrence Robinson, and Jeanne Segal, Ph.D. Last updated: September 2020.

"Depression," World Health Organisation, http://www.who.int/mediacentre/factsheets/fs369/en/,

"It's not rocket science, improve your life and become a better version of yourself", Tracey Ward, https://www.traceyward.me and https://www.karmatimes.co.uk

Laughter Club: Tracey Ward B.A. www.karmatimes.co.uk

Guided Meditation Recordings: Tracey Ward B.A., www.traceyward.me January 2021

A Darker Shade of Blue

Printed in Great Britain
by Amazon